THE NORTH AMERICAN MARIA THUN BIODYNAMIC ALMANAC 2019

CREATED BY
MARIA AND MATTHIAS THUN

Floris Books

Compiled by Matthias Thun
Translated by Bernard Jarman
Additional astronomical material
by Wolfgang Held and Christian Maclean

Published in German under the title *Aussaattage*
English edition published by Floris Books

British Library CIP Data available

ISBN 978-178250-531-0
ISSN: 2052-577X

Printed in China
through Asia Pacific Offset Ltd

Walther Thun, Mountain Stream, *1980 (oil, 55 x 87 cm)*

Introduction

Matthias Thun

Looking back over 2018 we were taken aback by the transition that occurred between winter 2017/18 and spring 2018. From our reading of the planetary constellations we had expected very mixed weather during the spring and no real winter. In the past it was usually the case in our geographic region that for a brief period in November temperatures would fall as low as –15°C (5°F). Later on it would get warmer again but the children could always look forward to snow at Christmas. By mid January it usually melted away. Winter then returned and did credit to its name for a further two to three weeks in mid February.

In 2018 we had several warm days in January during which the bees could undertake their cleansing flights. But then through into February, sunny and cold frosty days alternated with one another. In March this led to significant and frequent falls of snow. It was not easy for the bees to survive this period. Nature simply didn't want to wake up from her winter sleep. Somewhat friendlier night time temperatures arrived in April but it was the middle of the month before we experienced any real spring time temperatures.

We pondered long on why the planetary effects which we had so long been aware of, could not assert themselves. I then suddenly remembered the 1970s. At that time we had made similar observations. Periods of coldness occurred which could not have been caused by the known planets. These periods moved forward slowly and were confirmed by observers from completely different regions.

Maria Thun was convinced that it had to do with a heavenly body or planet which had not yet been discovered. After observing this phenomenon for many years she gave it the name Ringall, the one that encompasses the circle of planets. This may be an explanation for our own incorrect weather prediction. We intend to observe this further in future.

Brief Tips for Growing Different Plants

Maria Thun

Oil fruits

Sunflowers, linseed, rape and all other oil plants are best sown at Fruit times but later cultivation work and the spraying of horn silica is best carried out at Flower times. These treatments encourage copious oil production. Olives are given a horn silica spray immediately after blossoming on the whole tree.

Clockwise from top left:
Olive trees at Sekem, Egypt;
Sunflowers; Linseed.

Roses

In the fall it is good to apply well-rotted stinging nettle compost made the previous May to the soil where roses are to be planted.

An evening spraying of stinging nettle tea early in the year on the leaves at Leaf times strengthens the plants and keeps pests at bay. If garden chafers become a problem and damage the flowers a few specimens should be collected and burnt in a wood fire when the Sun and Moon are both in Taurus (May/June). The ashes should then be sprinkled beneath the roses.

Summer flowers

Summer annuals are sown and cultivated at Flower times. If a seed harvest is wanted, Fruit times should chosen later in the growth cycle.

Cabbage

Cabbage should follow legumes in the rotation; that is, after beans, peas, lentils or catch crops like lupins. It is a heavy feeder which means it thrives on rich compost. Well-composted cow manure applied the previous fall is best and ensures that no new fungal growths develop in the soil in springtime, otherwise all kinds of diseases might affect the plants later on. All of the cabbage family thrive when Leaf times are used for sowing and cultivation. There is one exception and that is broccoli, which prefers Flower times. Brussels sprouts and curly kale can be left over winter in the ground until ready to use. Other varieties need to be stored in the cellar or clamp over winter. It is wise not to harvest them at Leaf times otherwise they will not keep well. Flower or Fruit times should be chosen for this purpose. Flower and Fruit times should also be chosen when making Sauerkraut.

Cauliflower

Broccoli

Kohlrabi *Brussels sprouts* *Kale*

Cabbage *Sauerkraut*

7

Beans

For pole beans, dwarf beans and soya beans, Fruit times should be chosen for sowing, hoeing and treating with horn silica. This produces the best fruits. When sown at Root times there is a tendency for aphid attack especially on the underside of leaves. Horn silica needs to be sprayed at Fruit times shortly after sunrise.

Pole beans

Dwarf beans

Cucumbers

Cucumbers, zucchini, melons and pumpkins should be sown and hoed at Fruit times and horn silica should be given early in the morning before the flowers open.

Zucchini

Melons

The herb garden

If you wish to harvest the leaves of herbs, carry out sowing and cultivations at Leaf times. If the plants are to produce etheric oils, apply horn silica early in the morning at Flower times. Fennel, coriander and aniseed are cultivated at Fruit times so as to encourage seed formation.

Dill

A herb garden

Mirabelle plums

The trees carrying these six different fruits were all grown from the seeds of yellow mirabelle plum that were sown under six different planetary aspects. New trees have now grown from these fruits and retain the different colours and flavours.

Mirabelle plums

A selection of fruits

Raspberry with a bee

Blackberry with a bee

Hawthorn berry teas help heart circulation

Sloes can be made into a fine elixir to heal colds

Wild pear teas stimulate kidney activity

Elderflower tea reduces fever

Wild fruits

Around the edges of the fields of our trial plots, many kinds of wild fruits are growing. There are for instance raspberries and blackberries, which of course we often harvest and use at home.

Potatoes

If tubers left in the ground after the previous year's potato harvest are allowed to grow amongst the following crop, there is a danger of potato beetles appearing. The plants are weak and this is what potato beetles like. Healthy potatoes require a good crop rotation and well rotted compost applied to the soil the previous fall.

Fifty years ago plant breeders focused their energies on developing better potatoes. They were, however, concerned less with strengthening the whole plant than making better use of nitrogen fertilizers. Potato health was sacrificed to fertilizers. I still remember as a child how potato land was treated with manure and compost in the fall and how my father insisted on planting and hoeing only during fine weather.

In 1963 we began potato trials using cosmic rhythms and biodynamic preparations. On the areas designated for potatoes in our crop rotation we gave an fall application of two tons of well rotted manure compost. The compost is best worked into the surface of the soil in September together with a spraying of barrel preparation. The ground should be plowed and ready for the winter by the end of October. A further application of barrel preparation can accompany the plow.

Potato field

A plant with potato beetles

As soon as the soil warms up in spring it is cultivated at a Root time and sprayed with horn manure and barrel preparation. Then the potatoes are planted. In colder areas it is best to wait until the Sun has moved into Taurus (mid May). The potatoes will then germinate quickly and grow strongly. After about four weeks the potatoes should be sprayed twice in the evenings with stinging nettle tea at Leaf times.

Three times during the following weeks horn silica should be sprayed early in the morning at Root times. All the necessary cultivations including ridging up should always be carried out at Root times. If in the fall the potato tops have not died down sufficiently, an application of horn silica can be given at Root times in the afternoon. The harvest should also be carried out at Root times. With this treatment we have never had any problems with phytophtera, potato blight, and obtain good yields.

Some growers have problems with the Colorado beetle. The beetles should be collected up and stored in a glass jar with a lid until next spring. They should then be burnt when both Sun and Moon are in Taurus, potentized to D8 and sprayed three times when the Moon is in Taurus (for further details of ashing, see page 22). It can also be applied in the fall on ground where the next season's potatoes will be grown when it is plowed.

Tomatoes

Tomatoes belong to the group of plants known as heavy feeders. It is, however, not a plant that needs feeding large quantities of manure. In an answer to a question during the Agriculture Course, Rudolf Steiner said that the tomato would prefer above all to grow in its own compost.

We have undertaken many different trials with tomatoes. During our research work we have however been unable to confirm this particular indication.

Planting potatoes

Flowering potatoes

Working with potatoes   *Tomatoes*

We have gathered the tomato halms in the fall and composted them using the biodynamic compost preparations and then used this compost for the tomato bed the following spring. We then compared the results with manure compost and general plant compost.

The tomatoes which had received the equivalent of 1 ton of manure compost in the fall produced the best and healthiest plants and with very good yields. Those which had only received plant compost appeared under-nourished even though hoof and horn meal had been added to the compost. The plants grown in their own compost suffered fungal attacks already in early growth stages.

With every sowing, whether in the greenhouse, on the window-sill or when planting outdoors, an application of horn manure is given.

In the crop rotation tomatoes can follow the cabbage family. As soon as the plants have their third pair of leaves they are given an evening spray of nettle tea. This is repeated three times during the course of one month. On the following Fruit times horn silica is stirred early in the morning and sprayed on the plants, also three times within a month.

Side shoots should be removed at Fruit times towards evening. All such work on the plants should be undertaken at Fruit times. The fruit is best picked on Fruit and Flower times avoiding the unfavourable blanked out times.

To collect seed, fruit should selected by the end of September and not the last ones growing at the end of November. If, when the time comes for clearing away the plants, some good green fruits are still hanging, the whole plants can be pulled out of the earth with their roots and hung upside down in a sunny place. The fruits will then still ripen sufficiently to serve for supper.

With the triple applications of nettle tea and horn silica, the leaf surfaces will be strengthened to such an extent that no spores of blight will be able to gain a foothold. If there are late frosts after the tomatoes have been planted outside, ten drops of valerian can be stirred for ten minutes in ten litres (2½ gal) of water and sprayed on them. The leaves usually hang wilted for a while afterwards. A spraying of stinging nettle tea should then be given to both plants and soil followed by a thorough watering with clear fresh water. After a few hours the plants will be standing upright again and grow on normally.

Horn silica should be sprayed on top fruit and berries during summer in order to support bud development for the following year at Fruit times in late June and early July.

Companion Planting

We often receive letters from our readers asking why we never recommend any particular plant combinations in our publications. We have found after many years of research that our cultivated plants express a fourfoldness. This fourfoldness is expressed in the roots, leaves, flowers and in the fruit or seed. In taking account of the most strongly developed part of a given food-producing plant, namely that which is used for human food, there is a corresponding differentiation that is reflected in the passage of the Moon through the constellations of the zodiac. Based on these observations we have come to refer to Root times in relation to root produce, Leaf times in relation to leaf produce, Flower times for flowering plants and Fruit times for fruit and seed producing plants.

Because the desired qualities can be enhanced through the activity of hoeing and general care of the plants, it is not possible grow plants with different fruiting parts together. To do so would mean allowing one or the other crop to suffer.

As regards human nutrition, the plant provides five impulses. According to Rudolf Steiner substances from the root work on the brain and nervous system, those from the leaves affect the lungs and breathing, from the flowers the kidneys, the fruit the blood and from the seeds affect the human heart.

When we eat tomatoes we take in fruit and seed qualities, when we eat plums we take in fruit qualities and when we eat fennel, coriander or cumin we take in seed qualities. In our cultivation work the same sowing times are used for fruit and seed crops but in their later care the forces which come from Leo are especially important for seed formation.

A very clear example of the far-reaching importance of hoeing was demonstrated in a larger trial with spinach in the late 1960s. Around this time spinach became available as ready-made baby-food in jars. When this spinach was served in a children's hospital some small children suffered from nitrate poisoning. There was a huge outcry. A government institute undertook urgent research.

We were asked grow spinach using our understanding of baby nutrition. The seeds used in our trials came from the same institute. We prepared an area for the trial on our field in Gisselberg, which had had the same previous crop. Soil cultivation, seedbed preparation and the spraying of horn manure were all carried out at Leaf times. The next day, which was also Leaf time, the whole area was sown with spinach using a small sowing machine.

The area was later divided into different plots:

- Six beds were hoed at Leaf times, and three of these were sprayed with horn silica at Leaf times.
- Six beds were hoed at Flower times, and three of these were sprayed with horn silica at Flower times.
- Six beds were hoed at Fruit times, and three of these were sprayed with horn silica at Fruit times.
- Six beds were hoed at Root times, and three of these were sprayed with horn silica at Root times.

Spinach trials comparing hoeing

There were 24 beds in total. When the leaves were well developed the crop from each bed was harvested and carefully labelled. The institute then collected it for analysis. After some time the professor at the research institute phoned me up and said: 'Frau Thun, I had understood that you were using biodynamic methods. I find however that six of your variants have unusually high nitrate values and are totally unsuited for baby food!'

I was shocked at this, asked him for the numbers of those samples and set about checking them through.

As mentioned earlier, the preceding crop for all the variants was the same and all the seeds were sown on the same day. Those variants which were hoed at Root times, including those which had in addition received horn silica at Root times, were the ones which showed this poor quality. The best variants in every way were those that had been hoed and sprayed at Leaf times.

Soil analysis carried out in subsequent hoeing trials confirmed that soil bacteria fix more nitrogen when hoeing is carried out at Root times than at other times. As a result of this experience we have moved away from growing mixed cultures on the same bed. Small paths should always be made between the different plant types.

I remember those who introduced the idea of companion planting into vegetable production some thirty years ago. Gertrud Franck, best known for her use of spinach as a green manure, believed that different species of vegetables would be mutually beneficial to one another if planted in close proximity in the same bed. This idea was briefly taken up by Hans Erven who had a research station in Remagen. Erven had developed a raised bed, Hügelbeet, system. These beds were basically compost piles planted up with crops. The plants grew enormous but could not be used for food due to their high nitrate content. His colleague Ursula Venatur was initially very enthusiastic about the idea of companion planting but later also moved away from it.

The Biodynamic Preparations

In lectures given at the beginning of the twentieth century, Rudolf Steiner spoke of how the earth is dying and will become a corpse, and that human beings will need to bring it to life again. Among the audience were a number of farmers who subsequently asked: "What can we as farmers do to help?" Rudolf Steiner promised to give a course on agriculture, which he then did in June 1924. We have often referred to this Agriculture Course in our calendar.

The biodynamic movement was born as a result of the recommendations given in those lectures. The compost preparations were created expressly to re-enliven the earth. To make them, several require carefully chosen animal organ materials which are taken and filled with certain medicinal herbs and placed in the earth during winter. In spring they are taken out and used to inoculate manure and plant compost which is then used to enliven the soil and so enable the plants growing in it to make better use of cosmic influences.

The compost preparations

In considering the biodynamic preparations we need to start with compost. We place five different fermented substances separately into the compost. They are made from the herbs yarrow, chamomile, stinging nettle, oak bark and dandelion. A sixth preparation, valerian, is added in liquid form and is sprayed over the finished compost.

These preparations make it possible for the compost to achieve an ordered breakdown and transformation of organic materials into lasting humus. Each of these preparations brings a particular cosmic impulse in the compost and

Various biodynamic preparations

Cow manure in a cow horn ready for burying to make horn manure spray

Chamomile flowers in cow intestines ready for burying

enables the soil treated with it to receive the influences of each planet. They provide a cosmic gateway through which planetary forces become accessible to growing plants.

Yarrow is responsible for the forces of Venus, chamomile for those of Mercury, stinging nettle for those of the Sun, oak bark for those of Mars, dandelion for those of Jupiter and valerian for those of Saturn. In this way we have created in the compost a tiny planetary system that will later provide a good home in the soil for our cultivated crops.

Modifying the preparations

Some years ago in the UK there was the widespread practice of feeding meat to ruminants. The animals got ill with BSE, had to be slaughtered and were then incinerated. There was a great fear that the disease might be transferred to humans. Soon afterwards BSE appeared on the continent of Europe too and the EU Commission decided that animal organ materials were a risk and could no longer be used. Butchers were instructed that all the internal organs of cattle should be immediately destroyed.

This of course affected biodynamic farmers particularly strongly. After all, what is biodynamic agriculture without being able to use cattle organs to make the compost preparations? We had worked with them for many decades and carried out numerous tests on them.

We set out to discover whether the organs of sheep, goats, or deer could achieve the same effect as those from cows. One would, of course, have needed far more animals since their organs would be much smaller. During earlier research we had discovered that the yarrow preparation mediates Venus forces, chamomile Mercury forces, oak bark Mars forces, and dandelion Jupiter forces. Through our long term involvement with trees we were also aware of their respective links to planets.

We therefore decided to find out whether compost preparations made using wood from these trees would be as effective as those made in the normal way. This meant of course that in the following year we had to make and test an endless number of compost piles. Afterwards we set up trials with many different plants including a neutral follow up planting so that the reproductive strength of the affected plants could be investigated. Further trials were needed beyond this, however, in order that through analytical comparisons we could find out whether we were going in the right direction.

Manuring trials

In 2004 we made the biodynamic compost preparations in two different ways. We made one set in the classical way using animal organ materials as covers. A second set we made by replacing the animal organs with sheaths from trees and using these for the compost. After doing this for two years we could begin to compare results.

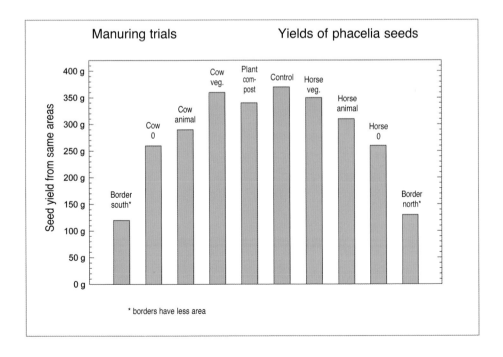

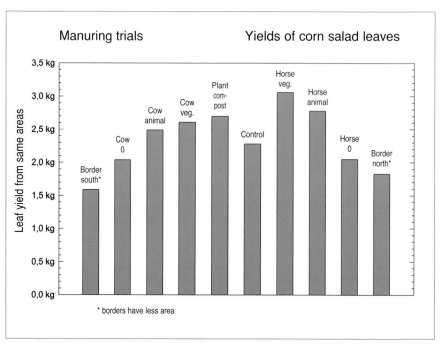

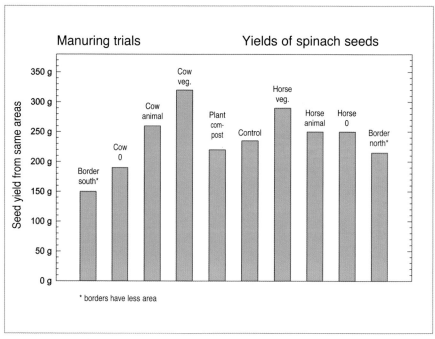

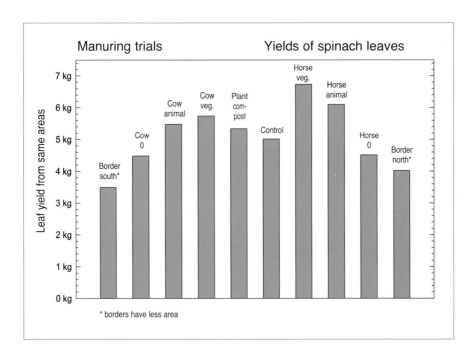

These diagrams show the yields of phacelia, corn salad, spinach and spinach seeds. It was amazing to see that in the case of both horse manure and cow manure the highest yields arose when they were treated with the so-called vegetarian preparations. This was very comforting to us in the face of current restrictions in the EU on the use of animal by-products. The four diagrams show these positive yield effects and could be a useful means for enabling farmers and gardeners affected by these restrictions to continue working bio-dynamically.

Animal and Insect Pests

The first question to ask is: Why does a particular animal appear as a pest? The first step is to familiarize oneself with the living conditions and habits of the creature in question and to rectify any management errors that have been made. If despite this an animal becomes a pest, it can be driven back to within its natural limits using its own burnt remains – its ashes. For details and timings see the monthly notes.

There is no need to reach for biological and chemical means of control; instead regulate the animal or insect from within its own species. For mice, birds and the like, a few skins or the feathers should suffice while for insects, slugs, etc. the following method should be followed:

Take 50 or 60 specimens of the particular pest and burn them in a wood fire during the appropriate planetary aspect. The resulting mixture of wood and pest ash should then be "dynamized" by grinding it in a mortar for an hour.

One gram of this dynamized ash should then be placed in a small bottle with 9 cc (grams) of water and shaken vigorously for three minutes. This is the first decimal potency (D1 or X1). A further 90 cc of water are then added and it is again shaken for three minutes. This is the second decimal potency, D2 or X2. Repeating this procedure until D8 (X8) would produce 100,000 litres (26,000 gallons). It is therefore advisable to proceed until D4 and then start again using smaller quantities (always diluting in the ratio of one to nine).

This D8 potency has been found to exhibit an inhibiting effect on the reproductive capacity of the pest when it is applied as a fine mist for three evenings in succession. Good results have been reported for several species. Where pests occur in large numbers good results are obtained by burning them on the site where they have been found. Flea beetle and apple blossom weevil can be caught with fly papers for example and burnt on site.

Ashing Wild Animal Skins

We always have many questions about this topic from our readers. In the woodland rich district where we live, the incursion of wild animals is a continuing threat to our trial beds. If fences are not dug at least half a metre into the ground, wild boar can easily lift them up while the roe and red deer simply leap over the top.

A hunter friend of ours gave us a skin. We burnt it in the wood oven at the time recommended in the calendar. The ash from the skin was then ground up

Burning skin in the wood oven   *Dynamizing the ash*   *Burning in the field*

together with the wood ash and dynamized for one hour using a pestle and mortar. A cement mixer can also be used. The skin ash was then potentized to D8 with the wood ash.

On one field the ash was sprinkled along the perimeter by hand. For a larger area, Matthias put the ash into a small sowing machine. Using a piece of rolled up paper he set the machine so that only a minute amount of ash was released. In this way all the fields could be sprayed in a continuous line without any break. We then compared the effect of dynamized ash with the D8 potency.

In both cases the animals remained away from our cultivated fields. The effect of the deer ash could be clearly observed on an unfenced clover field. The animals had grazed the clover in the surrounding fields but not within seven feet of the trial area. They had not crossed the line marked by the ash. Indeed the ash radiated its effect seven feet beyond it.

To dynamize the ash we take 100 g (4 oz) of skin ash and 900 g (36 oz) of wood ash and grind it for one hour or beginning with 10 g (⅓ oz) we potentize it to D8 with either wood ash or water. For the dry material we use the sowing machine. When mixed with water we use a knapsack sprayer and on large areas a tractor-mounted sprayer. We had far better results using a machine than when we simply sprinkled it by hand.

23

Background to the Calendar

The zodiac

The **zodiac** is a group of twelve constellations of stars which the Sun, Moon and all the planets pass on their circuits. The Sun's annual path always takes exactly the same line, called **ecliptic.** The Moon's and planets' paths vary slightly, sometimes above and sometimes below the ecliptic. The point at which their paths cross the ecliptic is called a **node** (☊ and ☋).

The angles between the Sun, Moon and planets are called **aspects.** In this calendar the most important is the 120° angle, or **trine.**

In the illustration below the outer circle shows the varying sizes of the visible **constellations** of the **zodiac.** The dates on this outer circle are the days on which the Sun enters the constellation (this can change by one day because of leap years). The inner circle shows the divisions into equal sections of 30° corresponding to the **signs** used in astrology.

It is the *constellations,* not the signs, on which our observations are based, and which are used throughout this calendar.

The twelve constellations are grouped into four different types, each having three constellations at an angle of about 120°, or trine. About every nine days the Moon passes from one type, for instance Root, through the other types (Flower, Leaf and Fruit) and back to Root again.

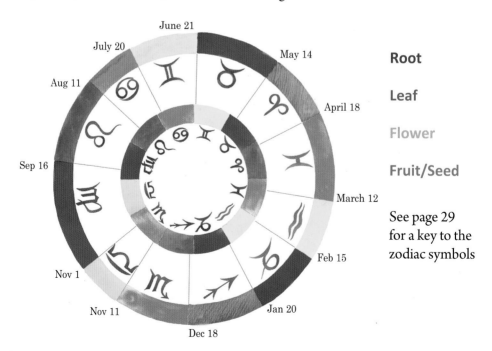

Root

Leaf

Flower

Fruit/Seed

See page 29
for a key to the
zodiac symbols

If a New Moon is at a node there is a solar eclipse, as the Moon is directly in front of the Sun, while a Full Moon at a node causes a lunar eclipse where the Earth's shadow falls on the Moon. If the Sun or Moon pass exactly in front of a planet, there is an occultation (☌). If Mercury or Venus pass exactly in front of the Sun, this is a transit (other planets cannot pass in front of the Sun).

What are oppositions, trines and conjunctions?
Oppositions ☍

A **geocentric** (Earth-centred) **opposition** occurs when for the observer on the Earth there are two planets opposite one another – 180° apart – in the heavens. They look at one another from opposite sides of the sky and their light interpenetrates. Their rays fall on to the Earth and stimulate in a beneficial way the seeds that are being sown in that moment. In our trials we have found that seeds sown at times of opposition resulted in a higher yield of top quality crops.

With a **heliocentric** (Sun-centred) **opposition** an observer would need to place themselves on the Sun. This is of course physically impossible but we can understand it through our thinking. The Sun is in the centre and the two planets placed 180° apart also gaze at each other but this time across the Sun. Their rays are also felt by the Earth and stimulate better plant growth. However, heliocentric oppositions are not shown or taken into account in the calendar.

At times of opposition two zodiac constellations are also playing their part. If one planet is standing in a Warmth constellation, the second one will usually be in a Light constellation or vice versa. If one planet is in a Water constellation, the other will usually be in an Earth one. (As the constellations are not equally sized, the point opposite may not always be in the opposite constellation.)

Trines △ or ▲

The twelve constellations are grouped into four different types, each having three constellations at an angle of about 120°, or trine. About every nine days the Moon passes a similar region of forces.

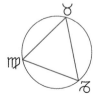
Earth-Root

Light-Flower

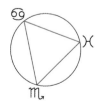
Water-Leaf

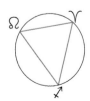
Warmth-Fruit/Seed

Trines occur when planets are 120° from one another. The two planets are then usually both standing in the same elemental configuration – Aries and Leo for example are both Warmth constellations. A Warmth trine means that the effects of these constellations will enhance fruit and seed formation in the plants sown at this time. If two planets are in trine position in Water, watery influences will be enhanced, which usually brings high rainfall. Plants sown at these times will yield more leaf than those at other times. Trine effects can change the way plants grow.

Conjunctions ☌

Conjunctions and multiple conjunctions occur when two or more planets stand behind one another in space. It is then usually only the planet closest to the Earth that has any influence on plant growth. If this influence is stronger than that of the sidereal Moon, cosmic disturbances can occur that irritate the plant and cause checks in growth. This negative effect is increased further when the Moon or another planet stands directly in front of another – an occultation (☽) or eclipse in the case of Sun and Moon. Sowing at these times will affect subsequent growth detrimentally and harm a plant's regenerative power.

The effects of the Moon

In its 27-day orbit round the Earth the Moon passes through the constellations of the zodiac and transmits forces to the Earth which affect the four elements: Earth, Light (Air), Water and Warmth (Fire). They in turn affect the four parts of the plant: the roots, the flower, the leaves and the fruit or seeds. The health and growth of a plant can therefore be stimulated by sowing, cultivating and harvesting it in tune with the cycles of the Moon.

These cosmic forces can also be harnessed in beekeeping. By opening and closing the bee 'skep' or box in rhythm with the Moon, the bees' activity is directly affected.

The table opposite summarises the effects of the movement of the Moon through the twelve constellations on plants, bees and the weather.

The amount of time the Moon spends in any constellation varies between two and four days. However, this basic framework can be disrupted by planetary oppositions which override the normal tendencies; equally, it may be that trine positions (see above) activate a different elemental force to the ones the Moon is transmitting. Times when the Moon's path or a planet's path intersects with the ecliptic (ascending ☊ or descending ☋ node; see page 29) are subject to mainly negative effects. These are intensified if there is an eclipse or occultation, in which case the nearer planet interrupts the influence of the distant one. Such times are unsuitable for sowing or harvesting.

Constellation	Sign	Element	Plant	Bees	Weather
Pisces, Fishes	♓ W	Water	Leaf	Making honey	Damp
Aries, Ram	♈ H	Warmth	Fruit	Gathering nectar	Warm/hot
Taurus, Bull	♉ E	Earth	Root	Building comb	Cool/cold
Gemini, Twins	♊ L	Light	Flower	Gathering pollen	Airy/bright
Cancer, Crab	♋ W	Water	Leaf	Making honey	Damp
Leo, Lion	♌ H	Warmth	Fruit	Gathering nectar	Warm/hot
Virgo, Virgin	♍ E	Earth	Root	Building comb	Cool/cold
Libra, Scales	♎ L	Light	Flower	Gathering pollen	Airy/bright
Scorpio, Scorpion	♏ W	Water	Leaf	Making honey	Damp
Sagittarius, Archer	♐ H	Warmth	Fruit	Gathering nectar	Warm/hot
Capricorn, Goat	♑ E	Earth	Root	Building comb	Cool/cold
Aquarius, Waterman	♒ L	Light	Flower	Gathering pollen	Airy/bright

Groupings of plants for sowing and harvesting

When we grow plants, different parts are cultivated for food. We can divide them into four groups.

Root crops at Root times

Radishes, swedes, sugar beet, beetroot, celeriac, carrot, scorzonera, etc., fall into the category of root plants. Potatoes and onions are included in this group too. Root times produce good yields and top storage quality for these crops.

Leaf plants at Leaf times

The cabbage family, lettuce, spinach, lambs lettuce, endive, parsley, leafy herbs and fodder plants are categorised as leaf plants. Leaf times are suitable for sowing and tending these plants but not for harvesting and storage. For this (as well as harvesting of cabbage for sauerkraut) Fruit and Flower times are recommended.

Flower plants at Flower times

These times are favourable for sowing and tending all kinds of flower plants but also for cultivating and spraying 501 (a biodynamic preparation) on oil-bearing plants such as linseed, rape, sunflower, etc. Cut flowers have the strongest scent and remain fresh for longer if cut at Flower times, and the mother plant will provide many new side shoots. If flowers for drying are harvested at Flower times they retain the most vivid colours. If cut at other times they soon lose their colour. Oil-bearing plants are best harvested at Flower times.

Fruit Plants at Fruit times

Plants that are cultivated for their fruit or seed belong to this category, including beans, peas, lentils, soya, maize, tomatoes, cucumber, pumpkin, zucchini, but also cereals for summer and winter crops. Sowing oil-bearing plants at Fruit times provides the best yields of seeds. The best time for extraction of oil later on is at Flower times. Leo times are particularly suitable to grow good seed. Fruit plants are best harvested at Fruit times. They store well and their seeds provide good plants for next year. When storing fruit, also remember to choose the time of the ascending Moon.

There is always uncertainty as to which category some plants belong (see list on p. 57). Onions and beetroot provide a similar yield when sown at Root and Leaf times, but the keeping quality is best from Root times. Kohlrabi and cauliflowers belong to Leaf times, as does Florence fennel. Broccoli is more beautiful and firmer when sown at Flower times.

Explanations of the Calendar Pages

Next to the date is the constellation (and time of entry) in which the Moon is positioned. This is the astronomical constellation, not the astrological sign (see page 24). The next column shows solar and lunar events.

A further column shows which element is dominant on that day (this is useful for beekeepers). Note H is used for warmth (heat). Sometimes there is a change during the day; in this case, both elements are mentioned. Warmth effects on thundery days are implied but are not mentioned in this column, but may have a ♄ symbol in the far right 'Weather' column.

The next column shows in colour the part of the plant which will be enhanced by sowing or cultivation on that day. Numbers indicate times of day. On the extreme right, special events in nature are noted as well as anticipated weather changes which disturb or break up the overall weather pattern.

When parts of the plant are indicated that do not correspond to the Moon's position in the zodiac (often it is more than one part on the same day), it is not a misprint, but takes account of other cosmic aspects which overrule the Moon-zodiac pattern and have an effect on a different part of the plant.

Unfavourable times are marked thus ▬. These are caused by eclipses, nodal points of the Moon or the planets or other aspects with a negative influence; they are not elaborated upon in the calendar. If one has to sow at unfavourable times for practical reasons, one can choose favourable times for hoeing, which will improve the plant.

The position of the planets in the zodiac is shown in the box below, with the date of entry into a new constellation. R indicates the planet is moving retrograde (with the date when retrograde begins), D indicates the date when it moves in direct motion again.

On the opposite calendar page astronomical aspects are indicated. Those visible to the naked eye are shown in **bold** type. Visible conjunctions (particularly Mercury's) are not always visible from all parts of the Earth.

Astronomical symbols

Constellations		*Planets*		*Aspects*			
♓	Pisces	☉	Sun	☊	Ascending node	**St**	Storms likely
♈	Aries	☾,☽	Moon	☋	Descending node	♄	Thunder likely
♉	Taurus	☿	Mercury	⌢	Highest Moon	**Eq**	Earthquakes
♊	Gemini	♀	Venus	⌣	Lowest Moon	**Tr**	Traffic dangers
♋	Cancer	♂	Mars	**Pg**	Perigee	**Vo**	Volcanic activity
♌	Leo	♃	Jupiter	**Ag**	Apogee		Northern Trans-
♍	Virgo	♄	Saturn	☍	Opposition		planting Time
♎	Libra	♅	Uranus	☌	Conjunction		
♏	Scorpio	♆	Neptune	☄	Eclipse/occultation		Southern Trans-
♐	Sagittarius	♇	Pluto	☄•	Lunar eclipse		planting Time
♑	Capricorn	○	Full Moon	△	Trine (or ▲)		
♒	Aquarius	●	New Moon	E Earth	L Light/Air	W Water	H Warmth/Heat

Transplanting times

From midwinter through to midsummer the Sun rises earlier and sets later each day while its path across the sky ascends higher and higher. From midsummer until midwinter this is reversed, the days get shorter and the midday Sun shines from an ever lower point in the sky. This annual ascending and descending of the Sun creates our seasons. As it ascends and descends during the course of the year the Sun is slowly moving (from an Earth-centred point of view) through each of the twelve constellations of the zodiac in turn. On average it shines for one month from each constellation.

In the northern hemisphere the winter solstice occurs when the Sun is in the constellation of Sagittarius and the summer solstice when it is in Gemini. At any point from Sagittarius to Gemini the Sun is ascending, while from Gemini to Sagittarius it is descending. In the southern hemisphere this is reversed.

The Moon (and all the planets) follow approximately the same path as the Sun

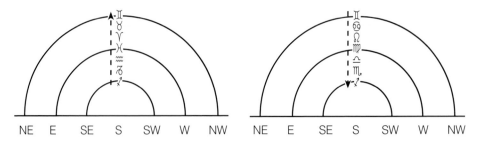

Northern hemisphere ascending Moon (left) and descending Moon (right): Transplanting Time

around the zodiac but instead of a year, the Moon takes only about 27 ½ days to complete one cycle, shining from each constellation in turn for a period of two to three days. This means that the Moon will ascend for about fourteen days and then descend.

It is important to distinguish the journey of the Moon through the zodiac (siderial rhythm) from the waxing and waning (synodic) cycle: in any given constellation there may be a waxing, waning, full, quarter, sickle or gibbous Moon. As it moves through the zodiac the Moon, like the Sun, is ascending (in the northern hemisphere) when it is in the constellations from Sagittarius to Gemini and descending from Gemini to Sagittarius. In the southern hemisphere it is ascending from Gemini to Sagittarius and descending from Sagittarius to Gemini.

When the Moon is ascending, plant sap rises more strongly. The upper part of the plant fills with sap and vitality. This is a good time for cutting scions (for grafting). Fruit harvested during this period remains fresh for longer when stored.

When the Moon is descending, plants take root readily and connect well with their new location. This period is referred to as the **Transplanting Time.** Moving plants from one location to another is called *transplanting*. This is the case when young plants are moved from the seed bed into their final growing position but also when the gardener wishes to strengthen the root development of young fruit trees, shrubs or pot plants by frequently re-potting them. Sap movement is slower during the descending Moon. This is why it is a good time for trimming hedges, pruning trees and felling timber as well as applying compost to meadows, pastures and orchards.

Note that sowing is the moment when a seed is put into the soil; either the ascending or descending period can be used. It then needs time to germinate and grow. This is different from *transplanting*, which is best done during the descending Moon. These times given in the calendar. Northern Transplanting Times refer to the northern hemisphere, and **Southern Transplanting Times** refer to the southern hemisphere. All other constellations and planetary aspects are equally valid in both hemispheres.

Local times

Times given are *Eastern Standard Time* (EST), or from March 10 to Nov 2 *Eastern Daylight Saving Time* (EDT), with [a] or [p] after the time for am and pm.

Noon is 12_p and midnight is 12_a; the context shows whether midnight at the beginning of the day or at the end is meant; where ambiguous (as for planetary aspects) the time has been adjusted by an hour for clarity.

For different time zones adjust as follows:

Newfoundland Standard Time: add $1\frac{1}{2}^h$
Atlantic Standard Time: add 1^h
Eastern Standard Time: do not adjust
Central Standard Time: subtract 1^h
  For Saskatchewan subtract 1^h, but subtract 2^h from March 10 to Nov 2 (no DST)
Mountain Standard Time: subtract 2^h
  For Arizona subtract 2^h, but subtract 3^h from March 10 to Nov 2 (no DST)
Pacific Standard Time: subtract 3^h
Alaska Standard Time: subtract 4^h
Hawaii Standard Time: subtract 5^h, but subtract 6^h from March 10 to Nov 2 (no DST)

For Central & South America adjust as follows:

Argentina: add 2^h, but add 1^h from March 10 to Nov 2 (no DST)
Brazil (Eastern): Jan 1 to Feb 16 add 3^h; Feb 17 to March 9 add 2^h; March 10 to Oct 19 add 1^h; Oct 20 to Nov 2 add 2^h; from Nov 3 add 3^h.
Chile: Jan 1 to March 9 add 2^h; March 10 to May 11 add 1^h; May 12 to Aug 10 do not adjust; Aug 11 to Nov 2 add 1^h; from Nov 3 add 2^h.
Columbia, Peru: do not adjust, but subtract 1^h from March 10 to Nov 2 (no DST).
Mexico (mostly CST): subtract 1^h, but from March 10 to April 6, and from Oct 27 to Nov 2, subtract 2^h

For other countries use *The Maria Thun Biodynamic Calendar* from Floris Books which carries all times in GMT, making it easier to convert to another country's local and daylight saving time.

January 2019

All times in EST

Date	Const. of Moon		Solar & lunar aspects	Trines	Moon El'ment	Parts of the plant enhanced by Moon or planets	Weather
1 Tue	♎		☉-♐	☿☋	L		
2 Wed	♏	2^a			L/W	Leaf from 8^a	
3 Thu	♏			▲	W	Leaf (sp good from 3_p)	
4 Fri	♐	12_p			W/H	Leaf to 11^a (sp good to 4^a); Fruit from 12_p	St
5 Sat	♐		◡ 1_p ☉☌● 8_p		H	Fruit to 11^a	☌♄ Tr
6 Sun	♐		☋ 7_p		H	Fruit from 12^a to 3_p	
7 Mon	♑	12^a			H/E	Root from 12^a	
8 Tue	♑		**Ag** 11_p		E	Root to 2_p; Flower from 3_p	St
9 Wed	♒	8^a			E/L	Fl 3^a; Rt 4-7^a; Flower from 8^a	Ч St
10 Thu	♒				L	Flower	St Vo
11 Fri	♓	11^a		☌♇	L/W	Fl to 4^a; Leaf from 11^a	
12 Sat	♓				W	Leaf	St
13 Sun	♓				W	Leaf to 11_a	St Vo
14 Mon	♈	1_p	☽ 2^a		W/H		St Vo
15 Tue	♈			♂☊	H	Fruit from 12_p	
16 Wed	♉	9^a			H/E	Fruit to 8^a; Root from 9^a	
17 Thu	♉				E	Root to 12^a	St Vo
18 Fri	♊	11_p	☉-♑	▲	E/L	Leaf 1^a to 3_p; Root 4_p to 10_p; 11	
19 Sat	♊		⌒ 6_p		L	Flower	Ч St Eq
20 Sun	♋	8_p	☊ 6_p		L/W	Flower to 3_p	Ч St
21 Mon	♋		☉☍○ 1^a **Pg** 3_p		W		St Eq Vo
22 Tue	♌	5^a			W/H	Fruit from 5^a	Tr
23 Wed	♌				H	Fruit	
24 Thu	♍	2_p			H/E	Fruit to 1_p; Root from 2_p	St Eq
25 Fri	♍			▲	E	1^a; Leaf from 2^a to 4_p; Root from 5_p	St
26 Sat	♍				E	Root	
27 Sun	♎	8_p	☾ 4_p		E/L	Root to 7_p; Flower 8_p	Tr
28 Mon	♎				L	Flower	
29 Tue	♏	6^a			L/W	Flower to 5_p; Leaf from 6^a	St Eq
30 Wed	♏				W	Leaf	
31 Thu	♐	6_p		☌♀	W/H	Leaf to 10^a; Fruit from 6_p	

NTT (1–5 Jan)

Northern Transplanting Time (19–31 Jan)

12 1 2 3 4 5 6 7 8 9 10 11 12 1 2 3 4 5 6 7 8 9 10 11 12

Mercury ☿	Venus ♀	Mars ♂	Jupiter ♃	Saturn ♄	Uranus ⛢	Neptune ♆	Pluto ♇
♏ 04 ♐	♎	♓	♏	♐	♓	♒	♐
23 ♑	04 ♏				(R 6 D)		

NB: All zodiac symbols refer to astronomical constellations, not astrological signs (see p. 24)

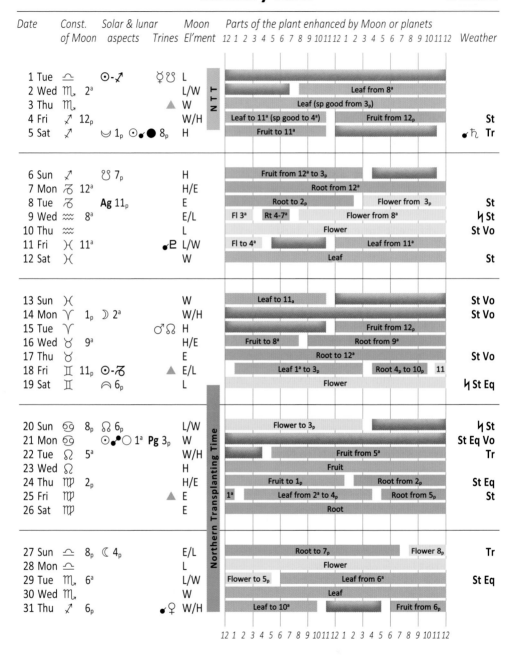

Planetary aspects

(**Bold** = *visible to naked eye*)

January 2019

1	☽☌♀ 5ₚ ☿♋ 7ₚ
2	☉☌♄ 1ᵃ
3	☽☌♃ 3ᵃ ☿△♁ 11ₚ
4	☽☌☿ 1ₚ
5	☽●♄ 2ₚ
6	☽☌♇ 7ᵃ
7	
8	
9	
10	☽☌♆ 8ₚ
11	☉●♇ 6ᵃ
12	☽☌♂ 7ₚ
13	☿☌♄ 9ᵃ
14	☽☌♁ 11ᵃ
15	♂♋ 1ᵃ
16	
17	☽☍♀ 3ₚ ☽☍♃ 10ₚ
18	♀△♂ 12ₚ ☿☌♇ 3ₚ
19	☽☍♄ 9ₚ
20	☽☍♇ 9ᵃ ☽☍☿ 2ₚ
21	
22	♀☌♃ 7ᵃ
23	☽☍♆ 10ₚ
24	
25	♂△♃ 1ₚ
26	☽☍♂ 4ᵃ
27	☽☍♁ 1ᵃ
28	
29	☉☌☿ 10ₚ
30	☽☌♃ 7ₚ
31	☽●♀ 1ₚ

With Jupiter in Scorpio, Venus joining it on January 5, and with Mars and Uranus in Pisces, the start of the year is likely to be quite wet. This is underpinned by the Water trines that are distributed throughout the month. We can however also hope for a mild January thanks to the presence of Mercury, Saturn and Pluto in the Warmth constellation of Sagittarius.

Northern Transplanting Time
Dec 23 to Jan 5 11ᵃ and
Jan 19 8ₚ to Feb 1
Southern Transplanting Time
Jan 5 3ₚ to Jan 19 4ₚ

The transplanting time is a good time for **pruning fruit trees, vines and hedges.** Fruit and Flower times are preferred for this work. Avoid unfavourable times.

Burn feathers or skins of **warm blooded pests** from Jan 16 3ₚ to Jan 18 9ₚ. Ensure the fire is glowing hot (don't use grilling charcoal). Lay dry feathers or skins on the glowing embers. After they have cooled, collect the light grey ash and grind for an hour with a pestle and mortar. This increases they efficacy and the ash can be potentized later. *The burning and grinding should be completed by Jan 18 9ₚ.*

When **milk processing** it is best to avoid unfavourable times. This applies to both butter and cheese making. Milk which has been produced at Warmth/Fruit times yields the highest butterfat content. This is also the case on days with a tendency for thunderstorms. Times of moon perigee (**Pg**) are almost always unfavourable for milk processing and even yoghurt will not turn out well. Starter cultures from such days decay rapidly and it is advisable to produce double the amount the day before. Milk loves Light and Warmth times best of all. Water times are unsuitable.

Planet (naked eye) visibility
Evening: Mars
All night:
Morning: Mercury (to 19th), Venus, Jupiter, Saturn (from 29th)

Unfavourable time

February 2019

Date	Const. of Moon	Solar & lunar aspects	Trines	Moon El'ment	Parts of the plant enhanced by Moon or planets 12 1 2 3 4 5 6 7 8 9 10 11 12 1 2 3 4 5 6 7 8 9 10 11 12	Weather

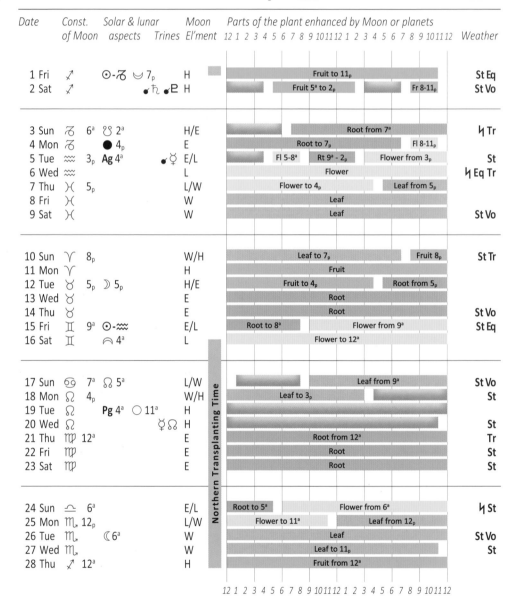

| 1 Fri | ♐ | ☉-♑ ☋ 7ₚ | | H | Fruit to 11ₚ | St Eq |
| 2 Sat | ♐ | | ● ♄ ● ♇ | H | Fruit 5ᵃ to 2ₚ Fr 8-11ₚ | St Vo |

3 Sun	♑	6ᵃ ☍ 2ᵃ		H/E	Root from 7ᵃ	♄ Tr
4 Mon	♑	● 4ₚ		E	Root to 7ₚ Fl 8-11ₚ	
5 Tue	♒	3ₚ Ag 4ᵃ	● ☿	E/L	Fl 5-8ᵃ Rt 9ᵃ - 2ₚ Flower from 3ₚ	St
6 Wed	♒			L	Flower	♄ Eq Tr
7 Thu	♓	5ₚ		L/W	Flower to 4ₚ Leaf from 5ₚ	
8 Fri	♓			W	Leaf	
9 Sat	♓			W	Leaf	St Vo

10 Sun	♈	8ₚ		W/H	Leaf to 7ₚ Fruit 8ₚ	St Tr
11 Mon	♈			H	Fruit	
12 Tue	♉	5ₚ ☽ 5ₚ		H/E	Fruit to 4ₚ Root from 5ₚ	
13 Wed	♉			E	Root	
14 Thu	♉			E	Root	St Vo
15 Fri	♊	9ᵃ ☉-♒		E/L	Root to 8ᵃ Flower from 9ᵃ	St Eq
16 Sat	♊	⌢ 4ᵃ		L	Flower to 12ᵃ	

17 Sun	♋	7ᵃ ☍ 5ᵃ		L/W	Leaf from 9ᵃ	St Vo
18 Mon	♌	4ₚ		W/H	Leaf to 3ₚ	St
19 Tue	♌	Pg 4ᵃ ○ 11ᵃ		H		
20 Wed	♌		☿ ☍	H		St
21 Thu	♍	12ᵃ		E	Root from 12ᵃ	Tr
22 Fri	♍			E	Root	St
23 Sat	♍			E	Root	St

24 Sun	♎	6ᵃ		E/L	Root to 5ᵃ Flower from 6ᵃ	♄ St
25 Mon	♏	12ₚ		L/W	Flower to 11ᵃ Leaf from 12ₚ	
26 Tue	♏	☾ 6ᵃ		W	Leaf	St Vo
27 Wed	♏			W	Leaf to 11ₚ	St
28 Thu	♐	12ᵃ		H	Fruit from 12ᵃ	

Northern Transplanting Time

12 1 2 3 4 5 6 7 8 9 10 11 12 1 2 3 4 5 6 7 8 9 10 11 12

Mercury ☿	Venus ♀	Mars ♂	Jupiter ♃	Saturn ♄	Uranus ♅	Neptune ♆	Pluto ♇
♑ 08 ♒	♏ 02 ♐	♓	♏	♐	♓	♒	♐
23 ♓	28 ♑	13 ♈			26 ♈		

NB: All zodiac symbols refer to astronomical constellations, not astrological signs (see p. 24)

Planetary aspects
(**Bold** = *visible to naked eye)*

1
2 **☾☌♄ 2^a** ☾☌♇ 3_p ♀△♅ 7_p
3
4
5 ☽☌☿ 2^a
6
7 ☽☌♆ 4^a
8
9
10 **☽☌♂ 4_p** ☽☌♅ 7_p
11
12
13 ♂☌♅ 1^a
14 ☽☍♃ 4_p
15
16 ☽☍♀ 9^a ☽☍♄ 1_p ☽☍♇ 10_p
17
18 **♀☌♄ 6^a**
19 ☿☌♆ 2^a
20 ☾☍♆ 10^a ☿☊ 11^a ☾☍☿ 2_p
21
22 ♀☌♇ 11_p
23 ☾☍♅ 10^a ☾☍♂ 10_p
24
25
26
27 **☾☌♃ 10^a**
28

Planet (naked eye) visibility
Evening: Mercury (from 14th), Mars
All night:
Morning: Venus, Jupiter, Saturn

February 2019

The beginning of the month will remain moist as Mars continues to reside in the Water constellation of Pisces until the middle of the month. This tendency is strengthened by Jupiter and Uranus and then later on furthered by Mercury. To begin with Mercury mediates some Light qualities and along with Neptune and Saturn, brings some warmth.

Northern Transplanting Time
Jan 19 to Feb 1 5_p and
Feb 16 6^a to Feb 28 10_p
Southern Transplanting Time
Feb 1 9_p to Feb 16 2^a

Vines, fruit trees and shrubs can be pruned during Transplanting Time selecting Flower and Fruit times in preference. Avoid unfavourable times.

Best times for taking **willow cuttings for hedges and fences:** At Flower times outside Transplanting Time. In warm areas at Flower times during Transplanting Time to avoid too strong a sap current.

Southern hemisphere harvest time for seeds
Always avoid unfavourable times.
Fruit seeds: Jan 31 6_p to Feb 2 11_p, and at other Fruit times.
Flower seeds: Feb 5 5^a to Feb 7 4_p, and at other Flower times.

Control slugs from Feb 17 9^a to Feb 18 3_p.

Unfavourable time

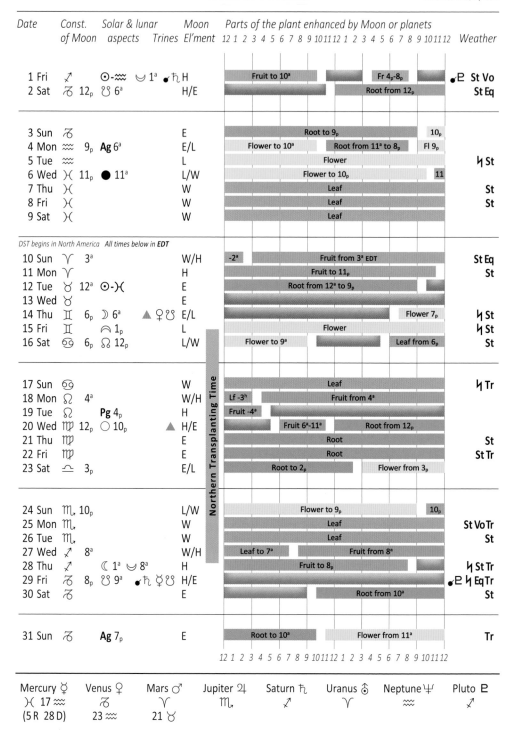

Date	Const. of Moon	Solar & lunar aspects	Trines	Moon El'ment	Parts of the plant enhanced by Moon or planets	Weather
1 Fri	♐	☉-♒	☍ 1ₐ • ♄ H		Fruit to 10ᵃ ... Fr 4ₚ-8ₚ	• ♇ St Vo
2 Sat	♑ 12ₚ	♌ 6ᵃ	H/E		Root from 12ₚ	St Eq
3 Sun	♑		E		Root to 9ₚ ... 10ₚ	
4 Mon	♒	9ₚ Ag 6ᵃ	E/L		Flower to 10ᵃ ... Root from 11ᵃ to 8ₚ ... Fl 9ₚ	
5 Tue	♒		L		Flower	♄ St
6 Wed	♓ 11ₚ	● 11ᵃ	L/W		Flower to 10ₚ ... 11	
7 Thu	♓		W		Leaf	St
8 Fri	♓		W		Leaf	St
9 Sat	♓		W		Leaf	

DST begins in North America All times below in EDT

Date	Const. of Moon	Solar & lunar aspects	Trines	Moon El'ment	Parts of the plant enhanced by Moon or planets	Weather
10 Sun	♈ 3ᵃ		W/H	-2ᵃ	Fruit from 3ᵃ EDT	St Eq
11 Mon	♈		H		Fruit to 11ₚ	St
12 Tue	♉ 12ᵃ	☉-♓	E		Root from 12ᵃ to 9ₚ	
13 Wed	♉		E			
14 Thu	♊ 6ₚ	☽ 6ᵃ	▲ ♀♌ E/L		Flower 7ₚ	♄ St
15 Fri	♊	⌒ 1ₚ	L		Flower	♄ St
16 Sat	♋ 6ₚ	♌ 12ₚ	L/W		Flower to 9ᵃ ... Leaf from 6ₚ	St
17 Sun	♋		W		Leaf	♄ Tr
18 Mon	♌ 4ᵃ		W/H	Lf -3ʰ	Fruit from 4ᵃ	
19 Tue	♌	Pg 4ₚ	H	Fruit -4ᵃ		
20 Wed	♍ 12ₚ	○ 10ₚ	▲ H/E		Fruit 6ᵃ-11ᵃ ... Root from 12ₚ	St
21 Thu	♍		E		Root	
22 Fri	♍		E		Root	St Tr
23 Sat	♎ 3ₚ		E/L		Root to 2ₚ ... Flower from 3ₚ	
24 Sun	♏ 10ₚ		L/W		Flower to 9ₚ ... 10ₚ	
25 Mon	♏		W		Leaf	St Vo Tr
26 Tue	♏		W		Leaf	St
27 Wed	♐ 8ᵃ		W/H		Leaf to 7ᵃ ... Fruit from 8ᵃ	
28 Thu	♐	☾ 1ᵃ ☍ 8ᵃ	H		Fruit to 8ₚ	♄ St Tr
29 Fri	♑ 8ₚ	♌ 9ᵃ • ♄ ☿ ♌	H/E			• ♇ ♄ Eq Tr
30 Sat	♑		E		Root from 10ᵃ	St
31 Sun	♑	Ag 7ₚ	E		Root to 10ᵃ ... Flower from 11ᵃ	Tr

(Northern Transplanting Time — vertical label along chart)

Mercury ☿	Venus ♀	Mars ♂	Jupiter ♃	Saturn ♄	Uranus ♅	Neptune ♆	Pluto ♇
♓ 17 ♒	♑	♈	♏	♐	♈	♒	♐
(5 R 28 D)	23 ♒	21 ♉					

NB: All zodiac symbols refer to astronomical constellations, not astrological signs (see p. 24)

Planetary aspects
(**Bold** = *visible to naked eye*)

March 2019

1	**☾☌♄** 1_p **☾☍♇** 11_p
2	**☾☌♀** 5_p
3	
4	
5	
6	☾☌♆ 12_p ☉☌♆ 8_p
7	☽☌☿ 2_p
8	
9	
10	☽☌☊ 4^a
11	☽☌♂ 11^a
12	
13	
14	☽☍♃ 6^a ♂△♄ 6^a ♀☋ 6^a ☉☌☿ 10_p
15	
16	☽☍♄ 2^a ☽☍♇ 9^a
17	
18	☽☍♀ 5^a
19	☽☍♆ 11_p
20	☽☍☿ 5^a ♂△♇ 8^a
21	
22	**☾☍☊** 11_p
23	
24	☿☌♆ 1_p **☾☍♂** 7_p
25	
26	**☾☌♃** 11_p
27	
28	
29	**☾☌♄** 1^a **☾☍♇** 8^a ☿☋ 9_p
30	
31	

Two Warmth trines and Saturn and Pluto – two warmth-bearing planets – in the Warmth constellation of Sagittarius, promise to make March a mild month. Towards the end of the month Venus and Mercury should also bring some Light.

Northern Transplanting Time
March 15 3_p to March 28 6^a
Southern Transplanting Time
March 1 2^a to March 15 11^a and
March 28 10^a to April 11

Willow cuttings for **pollen production** are best cut from March 23 3^a to March 24 9_p; and for **honey flow** from March 18 4^a to March 20, 11^a. Avoid unfavourable times.

Cuttings for grafting: Cut outside Transplanting Time during ascending Moon – always choosing times (Fruit, Leaf, etc.) according to the part of plant to be enhanced.

Control slugs: March 16 6_p to March 18 3^a.

Southern hemisphere harvest time for seeds
Always avoid unfavourable times.
Fruit seeds: March 10 3^a (EDT) to March 11 11_p, and at other Fruit times.
Flower seeds: Flower times.
Leaf seeds: Leaf times.
Root seeds: Root times.

Biodynamic preparations: Pick dandelion in March or April in the mornings during Flower times. The flowers should not be quite open in the centre. Dry them on paper in the shade, not in bright sunlight.

Planet (naked eye) visibility
Evening: Mercury (to 9th), Mars
All night:
Morning: Venus, Jupiter, Saturn

Unfavourable time

April 2019

April

Date	Const. of Moon	Solar & lunar aspects	Trines	Moon El'ment	Parts of the plant enhanced by Moon or planets	Weather

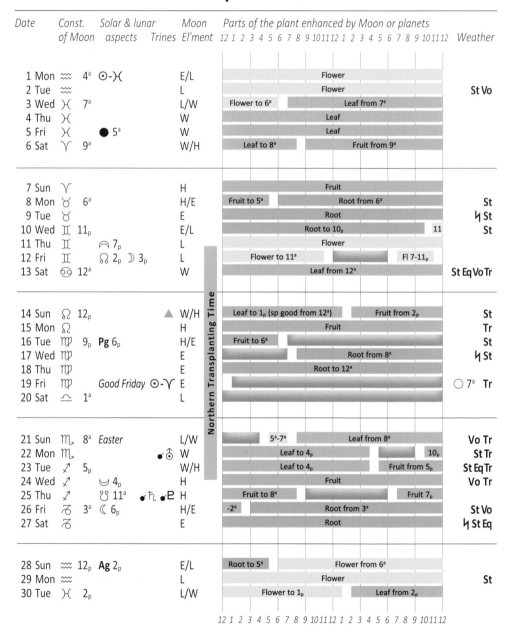

Date	Const. of Moon	Solar & lunar aspects	Trines	Moon El'ment	Parts of the plant enhanced by Moon or planets (12 1 2 3 4 5 6 7 8 9 10 11 12 1 2 3 4 5 6 7 8 9 10 11 12)	Weather
1 Mon	♒	4ᵃ ☉-)(		E/L	Flower	
2 Tue	♒			L	Flower	St Vo
3 Wed	)(	7ᵃ		L/W	Flower to 6ᵃ / Leaf from 7ᵃ	
4 Thu	)(			W	Leaf	
5 Fri	)(	● 5ᵃ		W	Leaf	
6 Sat	♈	9ᵃ		W/H	Leaf to 8ᵃ / Fruit from 9ᵃ	
7 Sun	♈			H	Fruit	
8 Mon	♉	6ᵃ		H/E	Fruit to 5ᵃ / Root from 6ᵃ	St
9 Tue	♉			E	Root	♄ St
10 Wed	♊	11ₚ		E/L	Root to 10ₚ / 11	St
11 Thu	♊	⚭ 7ₚ		L	Flower	
12 Fri	♊	☊ 2ₚ ☽ 3ₚ		L	Flower to 11ᵃ / Fl 7-11ₚ	
13 Sat	♋	12ᵃ		W	Leaf from 12ᵃ	St Eq Vo Tr
14 Sun	♌	12ₚ	▲	W/H	Leaf to 1ₚ (sp good from 12ᵃ) / Fruit from 2ₚ	St
15 Mon	♌			H	Fruit	Tr
16 Tue	♍	9ₚ **Pg** 6ₚ		H/E	Fruit to 6ᵃ	St
17 Wed	♍			E	Root from 8ᵃ	♄ St
18 Thu	♍			E	Root to 12ᵃ	
19 Fri	♍	Good Friday ☉-♈		E		○ 7ᵃ Tr
20 Sat	♎	1ᵃ		L		
21 Sun	♏	8ᵃ Easter		L/W	5ᵃ-7ᵃ / Leaf from 8ᵃ	Vo Tr
22 Mon	♏		⚡⚷	W	Leaf to 4ₚ / 10ₚ	St Tr
23 Tue	♐	5ₚ		W/H	Leaf to 4ₚ / Fruit from 5ₚ	St Eq Tr
24 Wed	♐	⚮ 4ₚ		H	Fruit	Vo Tr
25 Thu	♐	☊ 11ᵃ	⚫♄ ⚫♇	H	Fruit to 8ᵃ / Fruit 7ₚ	
26 Fri	♑	3ᵃ ☾ 6ₚ		H/E	-2ᵃ / Root from 3ᵃ	St Vo
27 Sat	♑			E	Root	♄ St Eq
28 Sun	♒	12ₚ **Ag** 2ₚ		E/L	Root to 5ᵃ / Flower from 6ᵃ	
29 Mon	♒			L	Flower	St
30 Tue	)(	2ₚ		L/W	Flower to 1ₚ / Leaf from 2ₚ	

Northern Transplanting Time

12 1 2 3 4 5 6 7 8 9 10 11 12 1 2 3 4 5 6 7 8 9 10 11 12

Mercury ☿	Venus ♀	Mars ♂	Jupiter ♃	Saturn ♄	Uranus ♅	Neptune ♆	Pluto ♇
♒	♒	♉	♏	♐	♈	♒	♐
9)(	13)(		(10 R)	(29 R)			(24 R)

NB: All zodiac symbols refer to astronomical constellations, not astrological signs (see p. 24)

Planetary aspects

(**Bold** = *visible to naked eye*)

1	
2	☾☌♀ 3ᵃ ☿☌♅ 6ᵃ ☾☌♅ 9ₚ ☾☌☿ 10ₚ
3	
4	
5	
6	☽☌⚷ 12ₚ
7	
8	
9	☽☌♂ 4ᵃ
10	♀☌♅ 2ᵃ ☽☌♃ 1ₚ
11	
12	☽☍♄ 11ᵃ ☽☍♇ 4ₚ
13	
14	☉△♃ 10ᵃ
15	
16	☽☍♅ 11ᵃ
17	☽☍♀ 1ᵃ ☽☍☿ 8ₚ
18	
19	☾☍⚷ 1ₚ
20	
21	
22	☾☍♂ 3ₚ ☉☌⚷ 7ₚ
23	☾☌♃ 8ᵃ
24	
25	☾☌♄ 11ᵃ ☾☌♇ 4ₚ
26	
27	
28	
29	
30	☾☌♅ 7ᵃ

The first half of the month promises to be quite bright, but when Mercury and Venus enter Pisces we can expect some rainy days. These are likely however to remain mild thanks to the presence in Sagittarius of the warming planets Saturn and Pluto.

Northern Transplanting Time
April 11 9ₚ to April 24 2ₚ
Southern Transplanting Time
March 28 to April 11 5ₚ and
April 24 6ₚ to May 8

Grafting of fruiting shrubs at Fruit times outside transplanting times.
   Grafting of flowering shrubs at Flower times outside transplanting times.

Control
Slugs from April 13 1ᵃ to April 14 1ₚ.
Clothes and wax moths from April 3 7ᵃ to April 6 8ᵃ.

Southern hemisphere harvest time for seeds
Always avoid unfavourable times.
Fruit seeds: Specially good from April 14 2ₚ to April 16 6ᵃ, and at other Fruit times.
Flower seeds April 10 11ₚ to April 12 11ₚ, and other at Flower times.
Leaf seeds at Leaf times, and **Root seeds** at Root times.

April

Planet (naked eye) visibility
Evening: Mars
All night: Jupiter
Morning: Venus, Saturn

Unfavourable time

May 2019

All times in EDT

Date	Const. of Moon	Solar & lunar aspects	Trines	Moon El'ment	Parts of the plant enhanced by Moon or planets (12 1 2 3 4 5 6 7 8 9 10 11 12 1 2 3 4 5 6 7 8 9 10 11 12)	Weather
1 Wed	♓	☉-♈		W	Leaf	St
2 Thu	♓		▲	W	Leaf (sp good from 3_p)	St Eq Vo
3 Fri	♈ 4_p			W/H	Leaf to 3_p (sp good to 4^a); Fruit from 4_p	
4 Sat	♈	● 7_p		H	Fruit	
5 Sun	♉ 1_p			H/E	Fruit to 12_p; Root from 1_p	
6 Mon	♉			E	Root	
7 Tue	♉			E	Root	St
8 Wed	♊ 5^a			E/L	Root -4^a; Flower from 5^a	St Eq
9 Thu	♊	⋒ 1^a ☊ 3_p	▲	L	Flower - 6^a; Leaf 7^a - 12_p; Fl 8_p	St Vo
10 Fri	♋ 6^a			L/W	Flower to 5^a; Leaf from 6^a to 5_p; Fruit from 6_p	St Eq
11 Sat	♌ 6_p	☽ 9_p	▲	W/H	Fruit to 8^a; Leaf 9^a to 5_p; Fruit from 6_p	
12 Sun	♌			H	Fruit	
13 Mon	♌	**Pg** 6_p	▲	H	Fruit to 6^a	St
14 Tue	♍ 5^a	☉-♉		H/E	Root from 7^a	
15 Wed	♍			E	Root	St
16 Thu	♍		▲	E	Root to 7^a; Fruit from 8^a from 10_p; 11	St
17 Fri	♎ 10^a			E/L	Root to 9^a; Flower 10^a-4_p; Fruit from 5_p	
18 Sat	♏ 6_p	○ 4_p	▲	L/W	Fruit to 6^a; 7^a-10^a	St
19 Sun	♏		☿☊	W		St
20 Mon	♏			W	Leaf from 12^a	
21 Tue	♐ 2^a			W/H	1^a; Fr 2^a - 6^a; Fruit from 12_p	St Eq Tr
22 Wed	♐	◡ 2^a ☋ 3_p	☌♄	H	Fruit to 12_p	
23 Thu	♑ 12_p		☌♇	H/E	Fruit from 3^a to 11^a; Root from 12_p	St
24 Fri	♑			E	Root	
25 Sat	♒ 8_p			E/L	Root to 7_p; Fl 8_p	St
26 Sun	♒	**Ag** 9^a ☾ 1_p		L	Flower	ϟ St
27 Mon	♓ 10_p			L/W	Flower to 9_p; 10_p	St
28 Tue	♓			W	Leaf	
29 Wed	♓			W	Leaf	St Vo
30 Thu	♓	*Ascension*		W	Leaf to 12^a	ϟ St Eq
31 Fri	♈ 1^a		▲	W/H	Fruit from 1^a (sp good from 5^a to 1_p)	

Northern Transplanting Time

12 1 2 3 4 5 6 7 8 9 10 11 12 1 2 3 4 5 6 7 8 9 10 11 12

Mercury ☿	Venus ♀	Mars ♂	Jupiter ♃	Saturn ♄	Uranus ♅	Neptune ♆	Pluto ♇
♓ 6 ♈	♓	♉	♏	♐	♈	♒	♐
18 ♉	14 ♈	15 ♊	(R)	(R)			(R)

NB: All zodiac symbols refer to astronomical constellations, not astrological signs *(see p. 24)*

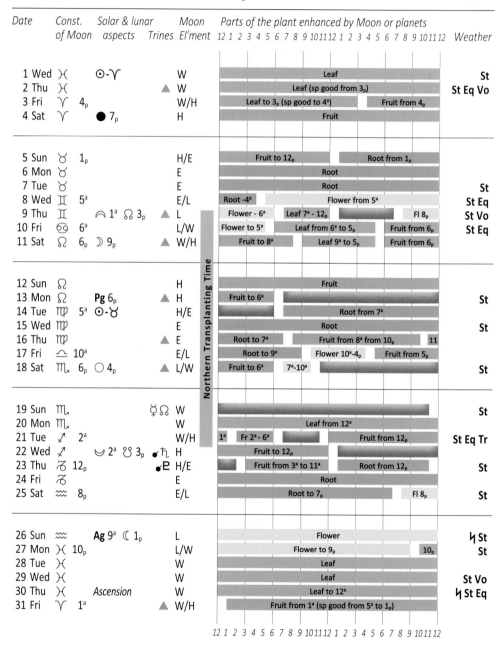

Planetary aspects
*(**Bold** = visible to naked eye)*

May 2019

1	
2	☾☌♀ 11ᵃ ☿△♃ 11ₚ
3	☾☌☿ 5ᵃ ☾☌♁ 10ₚ
4	
5	♂☍♃ 6ₚ
6	
7	☽☍♃ 5ₚ ☽☌♂ 8ₚ
8	☿☌♁ 10ᵃ
9	♀△♃ 1ₚ ☽☍♄ 5ₚ ☽☍♇ 9ₚ
10	
11	☉△♄ 5ᵃ
12	
13	☽☍♆ 7ₚ ☉△♇ 11ₚ
14	
15	
16	☿△♄ 7ₚ ☽☍♀ 9ₚ ☽☍♁ 11ₚ
17	
18	☿△♇ 2ᵃ ☽☍☿ 10ᵃ ♀☌♁ 12ₚ
19	☿♌ 11ᵃ
20	☾☌♃ 1ₚ
21	☉☌☿ 9ᵃ ☾☍♂ 11ᵃ
22	☾☍♄ 6ₚ
23	☾☍♇ 1ᵃ
24	
25	
26	
27	☾☌♆ 6ₚ
28	
29	
30	☿☍♃ 11ₚ
31	☾☌♁ 9ᵃ ♀△♄ 11ᵃ

Planet (naked eye) visibility
Evening: Mars
All night: Jupiter
Morning: Venus, Saturn

May is likely to be warm. Five Warmth trines will support the warming influence of Saturn, Uranus and Pluto and from later in the month Mercury and Venus as well. There may be some rainy days at the beginning of the month thanks to two Water trines and the presence of Mercury, Venus and Jupiter in Water constellations.

Northern Transplanting Time
May 9 3ᵃ to May 21 11ₚ
Southern Transplanting Time
April 24 to May 8 11ₚ and
May 22 4ᵃ to June 5

The **soil warms up** on May 7.

Transplant **table potatoes** at Root times.
Transplant **seed potatoes** for 2020 from May 3 4ₚ to May 5 12ₚ and from May 31 1ᵃ to June 1 8ₚ for small potatoes.

Hay should be cut between May 8 5ᵃ and May 9 6ᵃ, and at other Flower times.

Control:
Moths from May 27 10ₚ to May 30 11ₚ.
Flies by burning fly papers in the cow barn at Flower times.
Mole crickets ash from May 18 6ₚ to May 21 1ᵃ.

Begin **queen bee** rearing (grafting or larval transfer, comb insertion, cell punching) between May 8 5ᵃ and May 9 6ᵃ and at other Flower times.

Biodynamic preparations: The preparations can be taken out of the ground after May 12, avoiding unfavourable times. Preparations put into the ground after Sep 15, 2018, should wait to the end of May.

Maria Thun's tree log preparations: Cut **oak,** fill with coarsely ground oak bark and lay in the ground between May 5 1ₚ and May 6 4ᵃ. Cut **larch** logs, fill with chamomile and lay in the ground between May 30, 9ₚ and May 31 12ₚ.

Unfavourable time   41

June 2019

All times in EDT

Date	Const. of Moon	Solar & lunar aspects	Trines	Moon El'ment	Parts of the plant enhanced by Moon or planets (12 1 2 3 4 5 6 7 8 9 10 11 12 1 2 3 4 5 6 7 8 9 10 11 12)	Weather
1 Sat	♉ 9$_p$	☉-♉		H/E	Fruit to 8$_p$; Rt 9$_p$	
2 Sun	♉		▲	E	Root to 5$_p$; Fruit from 6$_p$	
3 Mon	♉	● 6^a		E	-2^a; Root from 3^a	
4 Tue	♊ 12$_p$			E/L	Root to 11^a; Flower from 12^a	St
5 Wed	♊	⋒ 8^a ☊ 7$_p$		L	Flower to 4$_p$	
6 Thu	♋ 12$_p$			L/W	Flower 12^a to 11^a; Leaf from 12$_p$	♄ St
7 Fri	♌ 11$_p$	**Pg** 7$_p$		W/H	Leaf to 7^a	St Vo
8 Sat	♌			H	Fruit from 8^a	
9 Sun	♌	*Pentecost*		H	Fruit	St Eq Tr
10 Mon	♍ 10^a	☽ 2^a		H/E	Fruit to 9^a; Root from 10^a	
11 Tue	♍			E	Root	
12 Wed	♍			E	Root	
13 Thu	♎ 5$_p$			E/L	Root to 2$_p$; Flower 3$_p$ (sp good)	
14 Fri	♎		▲	L	Flower to 12$_p$ (sp good to 4^a)	
15 Sat	♏ 1^a			L/W	Leaf from 1^a to 10$_p$; 11	♄ StVoTr
16 Sun	♏		▲	W	Flower to 12$_p$; Leaf from 1$_p$	St Eq
17 Mon	♐ 10^a	○ 4^a		W/H	Leaf to 9^a; Fruit from 10^a	
18 Tue	♐	◡11^a ☋10$_p$	☌♄	H	Fruit to 7$_p$	♄ St
19 Wed	♑ 8$_p$		☌♇	H/E	Fruit from 10^a to 7$_p$; Root 8$_p$	St
20 Thu	♑			E	Root	
21 Fri	♑	☉-♊		E	Root	St
22 Sat	♒ 4^a			E/L	Rt -3^a; Flower from 4^a	St Vo
23 Sun	♒	**Ag** 4^a		L	Flower	
24 Mon	♓ 6^a			L/W	Flower to 5^a; Leaf from 6^a	St Eq
25 Tue	♓	☾ 6^a		W	Leaf to 5$_p$	St
26 Wed	♓		☿☋	W		♄ St
27 Thu	♈ 9^a			W/H	Fruit from 9^a	
28 Fri	♈			H	Fruit	
29 Sat	♉ 6^a			H/E	Fruit to 5^a; Root from 6^a	
30 Sun	♉			E	Root	St

Northern Transplanting Time (5 Wed – 18 Tue)

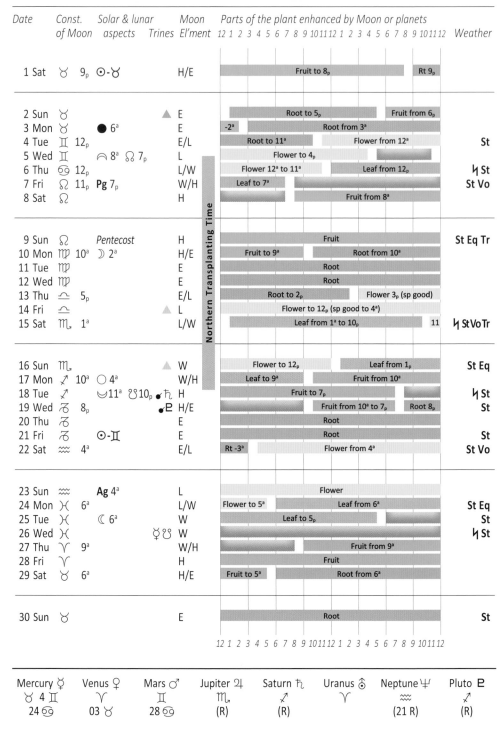

Mercury ☿	Venus ♀	Mars ♂	Jupiter ♃	Saturn ♄	Uranus ♅	Neptune ♆	Pluto ♇
♉ 4 ♊	♈	♊	♏	♐	♈	♒	♐
24 ♋	03 ♉	28 ♋	(R)	(R)		(21 R)	(R)

June

NB: All zodiac symbols refer to astronomical constellations, not astrological signs (see p. 24)

Planetary aspects
(**Bold** = *visible to naked eye*)

1 ☾☌♀ 4ₚ

2 ♀△♇ 11ₚ
3 ☽☍♃ 8ₚ
4 ☽☌☿ 12ₚ
5 ☽☌♂ 11ᵃ ☽☍♄ 9ₚ
6 ☽☍♇ 3ᵃ
7
8

9
10 ☽☍♆ 1ᵃ ☉☍♃ 11ᵃ
11
12
13 ☽☍⊕ 9ᵃ
14 ♂△♆ 2ᵃ ♂☍♄ 12ₚ
15 ☽☍♀ 8ₚ

16 ☿△♆ 8ᵃ ☿☍♄ 10ᵃ ☽☌♃ 3ₚ
17
18 ☿☌♂ 12ₚ ☾●♄ 11ₚ
19 ☾☌♂ 6ᵃ ☿☍♇ 7ᵃ ☾●♇ 7ᵃ ☾☌☿ 7ᵃ ♂☍♇ 11ₚ
20
21
22

23 ♀☍♃ 1ₚ ☾☌♆ 11ₚ
24
25
26 ☿℧ 6ₚ
27 ☾☌⊕ 9ₚ
28
29

30 ☾☍♃ 11ₚ

There is a mixed picture for June. There are Warmth and Light constellations and three Warmth or Light trines to support the influence of Mercury and Mars in Gemini and Neptune in Aquarius. At the end of the month Mars and Mercury move into Cancer and this along with the presence of Jupiter in Scorpio, might lead us to expect some rain. Whether the cooling effect of Venus in Taurus is able to counter the warming influences of Saturn, Uranus and Pluto, remains to be seen.

Northern Transplanting Time
June 5 10ᵃ to June 18 9ᵃ
Southern Transplanting Time
May 22 to June 5 6ᵃ and
June 18 1ₚ to July 2

Cut **hay** at Flower times.

Begin **queen bee** rearing at Fruit and Flower times, avoiding unfavourable times.

Control:
Chitinous insects, wheat weevil, Colorado beetle and varroa from June 1 9ₚ to June 4 11ᵃ.
Flies by burning fly papers in the cow barn from June 13 5ₚ to June 14 11ₚ, and at other Flower times.
Grasshoppers from June 22 4ᵃ to June 24 5ᵃ.

Biodynamic preparations
Maria Thun's tree log preparations: Cut **maple** logs and fill with dandelion and lay in the ground on June 10 between 6ᵃ to 5ₚ.

Planet (naked eye) visibility
Evening: Mercury (3rd to 27th), Mars (to 13th)
All night: Jupiter, Saturn
Morning: Venus

Unfavourable time

July 2019

Date	Const. of Moon	Solar & lunar aspects	Moon Trines	El'ment	Parts of the plant enhanced by Moon or planets	Weather

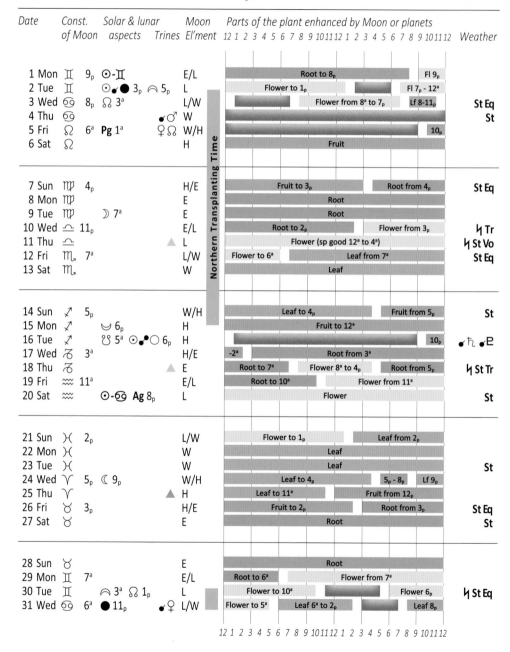

Vertical label: Northern Transplanting Time

Time scale: 12 1 2 3 4 5 6 7 8 9 10 11 12 1 2 3 4 5 6 7 8 9 10 11 12

1 Mon ♊ 9ₚ ☉-♊ — E/L — Root to 8ₚ — Fl 9ₚ
2 Tue ♊ ☉☽● 3ₚ ⌒ 5ₚ — L — Flower to 1ₚ — Fl 7ₚ - 12ᵃ
3 Wed ♋ 8ₚ ☽ 3ᵃ — L/W — Flower from 8ᵃ to 7ₚ — Lf 8-11ₚ — St Eq / St
4 Thu ♋ ☽♂ — W — Fruit
5 Fri ♌ 6ᵃ **Pg** 1ᵃ ♀♌ — W/H — 10ₚ
6 Sat ♌ — H — Fruit

7 Sun ♍ 4ₚ — H/E — Fruit to 3ₚ — Root from 4ₚ — St Eq
8 Mon ♍ — E — Root
9 Tue ♍ ☽ 7ᵃ — E — Root
10 Wed ♎ 11ₚ — E/L — Root to 2ₚ — Flower from 3ₚ — ♄ Tr
11 Thu ♎ ▲ — L — Flower (sp good 12ᵃ to 4ᵃ) — ♄ St Vo
12 Fri ♏ 7ᵃ — L/W — Flower to 6ᵃ — Leaf from 7ᵃ — St Eq
13 Sat ♏ — W — Leaf

14 Sun ♐ 5ₚ — W/H — Leaf to 4ₚ — Fruit from 5ₚ — St
15 Mon ♐ ☽ 6ₚ — H — Fruit to 12ₚ
16 Tue ♐ ☋ 5ᵃ ☉☽○ 6ₚ — H — 10ₚ — ♂♄ ♂♇
17 Wed ♑ 3ᵃ — H/E — -2ᵃ — Root from 3ᵃ
18 Thu ♑ ▲ — E — Root to 7ᵃ — Flower 8ᵃ to 4ₚ — Root from 5ₚ — ♄ St Tr
19 Fri ♒ 11ᵃ — E/L — Root to 10ᵃ — Flower from 11ᵃ
20 Sat ♒ ☉-♋ **Ag** 8ₚ — L — Flower — St

21 Sun ♓ 2ₚ — L/W — Flower to 1ₚ — Leaf from 2ₚ
22 Mon ♓ — W — Leaf
23 Tue ♓ — W — Leaf — St
24 Wed ♈ 5ₚ ☾ 9ₚ — W/H — Leaf to 4ₚ — 5ₚ - 8ₚ — Lf 9ₚ
25 Thu ♈ ▲ — H — Leaf to 11ᵃ — Fruit from 12ₚ
26 Fri ♉ 3ₚ — H/E — Fruit to 2ₚ — Root from 3ₚ — St Eq
27 Sat ♉ — E — Root — St

28 Sun ♉ — E — Root
29 Mon ♊ 7ᵃ — E/L — Root to 6ᵃ — Flower from 7ᵃ
30 Tue ♊ ⌒ 3ᵃ ☽ 1ₚ — L — Flower to 10ᵃ — Flower 6ₚ — ♄ St Eq
31 Wed ♋ 6ᵃ ● 11ₚ ♂♀ — L/W — Flower to 5ᵃ — Leaf 6ᵃ to 2ₚ — Leaf 8ₚ

Time scale: 12 1 2 3 4 5 6 7 8 9 10 11 12 1 2 3 4 5 6 7 8 9 10 11 12

Mercury ☿	Venus ♀	Mars ♂	Jupiter ♃	Saturn ♄	Uranus ⛢	Neptune ♆	Pluto ♇
♋ 22 ♊	♉ 03 ♊	♋	♏	♐	♈	♒	♐
(6 R 31D)	24 ♋	31 ♌	(R)	(R)		(R)	(R)

NB: All zodiac symbols refer to astronomical constellations, not astrological signs (see p. 24)

Planetary aspects
(**Bold** = *visible to naked eye)*

1 **☾☌♀ 6_p**
2
3 ☽☍♄ 3^a ☽☍♇ 10^a
4 ☽●♂ 2^a ☽☌☿ 6^a
5 ♀☊ 9^a
6

7 ☽☍♆ 7^a
8 ☿☌♂ 6_p
9 ☉☍♄ 1_p
10 ☽☍⛢ 4_p
11 ☉△♆ 1^a
12
13 **☽☌♃ 4_p**

14 ☉☍♇ 11^a
15
16 ☽☍♀ 1^a **☽●♄ 3^a** ☽●♇ 12_p
17 ♀☍♄ 2^a ☾☍☿ 8^a
18 ☾☍♂ 2^a ♀△♆ 2_p
19
20

21 ♀☍♇ 5^a ☉☌☿ 9^a ☾☌♆ 2_p
22
23
24 ☿☌♀ 8_p
25 ☾☌⛢ 6^a ♂△♃ 8^a
26
27

28 ☾☍♃ 5^a
29
30 ☾☍♄ 10^a ☾☍♇ 7_p ☾☌☿ 11_p
31 ☾●♀ 5_p

Planet (naked eye) visibility
Evening:
All night: Jupiter, Saturn
Morning: Venus (to 16th)

July 2019

There is a total eclipse of the Sun on July 2 (visible in the South Pacific and South America). It is likely to be rainy month with a Water trine and with Mars as well as Mercury, Jupiter and later on Venus all in Water constellations. Venus and two Light trines should however also ensure plenty of brightness.

Northern Transplanting Time
July 2 7_p to July 15 4_p and
July 30 5^a to Aug 11
Southern Transplanting Time
June 18 to July 2 3_p and
July 15 8_p to July 30 1^a

Late hay cut at Flower times.

Late hay cut at Flower times.

Summer harvest for seeds:
Flower plants: Harvest at Flower times, specially in the first half of the month.

Fruit plants from July 5 10_p to July 7 3_p, or at other Fruit times.

Harvest **leaf plants** at Leaf times.

Harvest **root plants** at Root times, especially July 7 4_p to July 10 2_p, and July 26 3_p to July 29 6^a.

Always avoid unfavourable times.

Control
Flies: burn fly papers in the cow barn at Flower times, avoiding unvafourable times.
Slugs: burn from July 3 8_p to July 5 5^a. Spray leaf plants and the soil with horn silica early in the morning during Leaf times.
Grasshoppers from July 19 11^a to July 21 1_p.

Biodynamic preparations
Maria Thun's tree log preparations: Birch should be cut (for yarrow flowers) and hung up on July 21 between 1^a and 9^a.

August 2019

Date	Const. of Moon	Solar & lunar aspects	Trines	Moon El'ment	Parts of the plant enhanced by Moon or planets	Weather

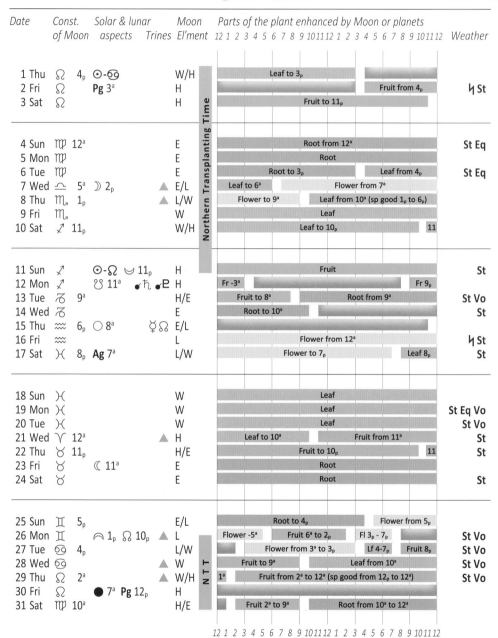

Image columns time scale: 12 1 2 3 4 5 6 7 8 9 10 11 12 1 2 3 4 5 6 7 8 9 10 11 12

Northern Transplanting Time

- **1 Thu** ♌ 4ₚ ☉-♋ — W/H — Leaf to 3ₚ
- **2 Fri** ♌ **Pg** 3ᵃ — H — Fruit from 4ₚ — ♄ St
- **3 Sat** ♌ — H — Fruit to 11ₚ

- **4 Sun** ♍ 12ᵃ — E — Root from 12ᵃ — St Eq
- **5 Mon** ♍ — E — Root
- **6 Tue** ♍ — E — Root to 3ₚ / Leaf from 4ₚ — St Eq
- **7 Wed** ♎ 5ᵃ ☽ 2ₚ ▲ — E/L — Leaf to 6ᵃ / Flower from 7ᵃ
- **8 Thu** ♏ 1ₚ ▲ — L/W — Flower to 9ᵃ / Leaf from 10ᵃ (sp good 1ₚ to 6ₚ)
- **9 Fri** ♏ — W — Leaf
- **10 Sat** ♐ 11ₚ — W/H — Leaf to 10ₚ — 11

- **11 Sun** ♐ ☉-♌ ☋ 11ₚ — H — Fruit — St
- **12 Mon** ♐ ☊ 11ᵃ ♄ ♇ — H — Fr -3ᵃ / Fr 9ₚ
- **13 Tue** ♑ 9ᵃ — H/E — Fruit to 8ᵃ / Root from 9ᵃ — St Vo
- **14 Wed** ♑ — E — Root to 10ᵃ — St
- **15 Thu** ♒ 6ₚ ○ 8ᵃ ☿♌ — E/L — E/L
- **16 Fri** ♒ — L — Flower from 12ᵃ — ♄ St
- **17 Sat** ♓ 8ₚ **Ag** 7ᵃ — L/W — Flower to 7ₚ / Leaf 8ₚ — St

- **18 Sun** ♓ — W — Leaf
- **19 Mon** ♓ — W — Leaf — St Eq Vo
- **20 Tue** ♓ — W — Leaf — St Vo
- **21 Wed** ♈ 12ᵃ ▲ — H — Leaf to 10ᵃ / Fruit from 11ᵃ — St
- **22 Thu** ♉ 11ₚ — H/E — Fruit to 10ₚ — 11 — St
- **23 Fri** ♉ ☾ 11ᵃ — E — Root
- **24 Sat** ♉ — E — Root — St

- **25 Sun** ♊ 5ₚ — E/L — Root to 4ₚ / Flower from 5ₚ
- **26 Mon** ♊ ⚹ 1ₚ ♌ 10ₚ ▲ — L — Flower -5ᵃ / Fruit 6ᵃ to 2ₚ / Fl 3ₚ - 7ₚ — St Vo
- **27 Tue** ♋ 4ₚ — L/W — Flower from 3ᵃ to 3ₚ / Lf 4-7ₚ / Fruit 8ₚ — St Vo
- **28 Wed** ♋ ▲ — W — Fruit to 9ᵃ / Leaf from 10ᵃ — St Vo
- **29 Thu** ♌ 2ᵃ ▲ — W/H — 1ᵃ / Fruit from 2ᵃ to 12ᵃ (sp good 12ₚ to 12ᵃ) — St Vo
- **30 Fri** ♌ ● 7ᵃ **Pg** 12ₚ — H —
- **31 Sat** ♍ 10ᵃ — H/E — Fruit 2ᵃ to 9ᵃ / Root from 10ᵃ to 12ᵃ

NTT

Time scale: 12 1 2 3 4 5 6 7 8 9 10 11 12 1 2 3 4 5 6 7 8 9 10 11 12

Mercury ☿	Venus ♀	Mars ♂	Jupiter ♃	Saturn ♄	Uranus ⛢	Neptune ♆	Pluto ♇
♊ 09 ♋	♋	♌	♏	♐	♈	♒	♐
23 ♌	12 ♌		(R 11 D)	(R)	(12 R)	(R)	(R)

NB: All zodiac symbols refer to astronomical constellations, not astrological signs (see p. 24)

Planetary aspects
(**Bold** = *visible to naked eye*)

1	☽ ☌ ♂ 5ₚ
2	
3	☽ ☍ ♅ 3ₚ
4	
5	
6	☽ ☍ ♃ 11ₚ
7	☉ △ ♃ 3ª
8	♀ △ ♃ 4ₚ
9	☽ ☌ ♃ 7ₚ
10	
11	
12	☽ ● ♄ 6ª ☽ ● ♇ 6ₚ
13	☽ ☍ ♀ 5ₚ
14	☉ ☌ ♀ 3ª
15	☽ ☍ ♀ 9ª ☿ ☊ 11ª ☾ ☍ ♂ 9ₚ
16	
17	☾ ☌ ♅ 12ₚ
18	
19	
20	
21	☿ △ ♃ 6ª ☾ ☌ ♁ 2ₚ
22	
23	
24	♀ ☌ ♂ 1ₚ ☾ ☍ ♃ 2ₚ
25	
26	♀ △ ♁ 12ₚ ☾ ☍ ♄ 6ₚ
27	☾ ☍ ♇ 5ª
28	♂ △ ♁ 7ª
29	☾ ☌ ☿ 10ₚ ☉ △ ♁ 11ₚ
30	☽ ☌ ♂ 8ª ☽ ☌ ♀ 2ₚ ☽ ☍ ♅ 11ₚ
31	

August 2019

August is dominated by Warmth constellations. They are reinforced by three Warmth trines at the end of the month. To begin with, however, Venus is in a Water constellation along with Jupiter and this together with three Water trines promises a moist start to the month. Mercury and Neptune though should bring some brightness.

Northern Transplanting Time
July 30 to Aug 11 10ₚ and
Aug 26 3ₚ to Sep 8
Southern Transplanting Time
Aug 12 2ª to Aug 26 11ª

Harvest **seeds of fruit plants** and **grain** to be used for seed from Aug 2 4ₚ to Aug 13 11ₚ, and at other Fruit times, avoiding unfavourable times.

Immediately after harvest, sow catch crops like lupins, phacelia, mustard or wild flax.

Seeds for leaf plants: harvest at Leaf times, specially in the second half of the month.

Seeds for flower plants: at Flower times, specially in the second half of the month.

Burn **fly papers** in the cow barn at Flower times.

Ants in the house: burn when the Moon is in Leo, Aug 1 4ₚ to Aug 3 11ₚ.

Aug

Planet (naked eye) visibility
Evening:
All night: Jupiter, Saturn
Morning: Mercury (5th to 25th)

Unfavourable time

September 2019

All times in EDT

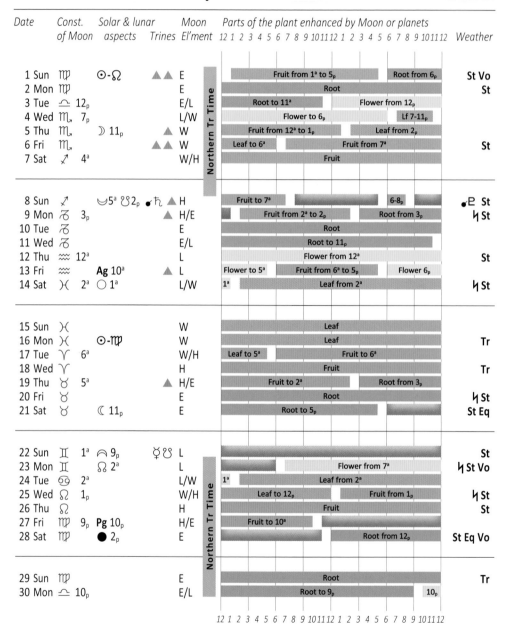

Date	Const. of Moon	Solar & lunar aspects	Trines	Moon El'ment	Parts of the plant enhanced by Moon or planets (12 1 2 3 4 5 6 7 8 9 10 11 12 1 2 3 4 5 6 7 8 9 10 11 12)	Weather
1 Sun	♍	☉-♌	▲▲	E	Fruit from 1a to 5p; Root from 6p	St Vo
2 Mon	♍			E	Root	St
3 Tue	♎ 12p			E/L	Root to 11a; Flower from 12p	
4 Wed	♏ 7p			L/W	Flower to 6p; Lf 7-11p	
5 Thu	♏	☽ 11p	▲	W	Fruit from 12a to 1p; Leaf from 2p	
6 Fri	♏		▲▲	W	Leaf to 6a; Fruit from 7a	St
7 Sat	♐ 4a			W/H	Fruit	
8 Sun	♐	◡5a ☋2p	●♄ ▲	H	Fruit to 7a; 6-8p	●♇ St
9 Mon	♑ 3p		▲	H/E	Fruit from 2a to 2p; Root from 3p	ϟ St
10 Tue	♑			E	Root	
11 Wed	♑			E/L	Root to 11p	
12 Thu	♒ 12a			L	Flower from 12a	St
13 Fri	♒	**Ag** 10a	▲	L	Flower to 5a; Fruit from 6a to 5p; Flower 6p	
14 Sat	♓ 2a	○ 1a		L/W	1a; Leaf from 2a	ϟ St
15 Sun	♓			W	Leaf	
16 Mon	♓	☉-♍		W	Leaf	Tr
17 Tue	♈ 6a			W/H	Leaf to 5a; Fruit to 6a	
18 Wed	♈			H	Fruit	Tr
19 Thu	♉ 5a		▲	H/E	Fruit to 2a; Root from 3p	
20 Fri	♉			E	Root	ϟ St
21 Sat	♉	☾ 11p		E	Root to 5p	St Eq
22 Sun	♊ 1a	◠ 9p	☿☋	L		St
23 Mon	♊	☊ 2a		L	Flower from 7a	ϟ St Vo
24 Tue	♋ 2a			L/W	1a; Leaf from 2a	
25 Wed	♌ 1p			W/H	Leaf to 12p; Fruit from 1p	ϟ St
26 Thu	♌			H	Fruit	St
27 Fri	♍ 9p	**Pg** 10p		H/E	Fruit to 10a	
28 Sat	♍	● 2p		E	Root from 12p	St Eq Vo
29 Sun	♍			E	Root	Tr
30 Mon	♎ 10p			E/L	Root to 9p; 10p	

Northern Tr Time

Mercury ☿	Venus ♀	Mars ♂	Jupiter ♃	Saturn ♄	Uranus ♅	Neptune ♆	Pluto ♇
♌	♌	♌	♏	♐	♈	♒	♐
10 ♍	09 ♍	24 ♍		(R 18 D)	(R)	(R)	(R)

NB: All zodiac symbols refer to astronomical constellations, not astrological signs (see p. 24)

Sep

Planetary aspects
*(**Bold** = visible to naked eye)*

1	☿△♆ 10ᵃ ♀△♄ 3ₚ
2	☉♂♂ 6ᵃ
3	☽♂♆ 6ᵃ ☿♂♂ 12ₚ ☉♂☿ 10ₚ
4	♀♂♆ 8ᵃ
5	☿△♄ 9ᵃ
6	☽♂♃ 3ᵃ ☉△♄ 6ₚ ♀△♇ 11ₚ
7	☿♂♆ 3ᵃ

8	☽♂♄ 10ᵃ ☽♂♇ 11ₚ ☿△♇ 11ₚ
9	♂△♄ 1ᵃ
10	☉♂♆ 3ᵃ
11	
12	
13	☿♂♀ 11ᵃ ☉△♇ 4ₚ ☽♂♂ 4ₚ ☽♂♆ 5ₚ
14	♂♂♆ 2ᵃ ☽♂♀ 8ₚ ☽♂☿ 9ₚ

15	
16	
17	☽♂♆ 7ₚ
18	
19	♂△♇ 12ₚ
20	
21	☽♂♃ 1ᵃ

22	☿♂ 6ₚ
23	☽♂♄ 2ᵃ ☽♂♇ 1ₚ
24	
25	
26	
27	☽♂♆ 9ᵃ ☽♂♂ 11ₚ
28	

29	☽♂♀ 12ₚ ☽♂☿ 10ₚ
30	☽♂♆ 3ₚ

The number of Warmth trines during the first half of the month is quite overwhelming. This and the fact that Mercury, Venus, Mars, Saturn Uranus and Pluto are in Warmth constellations will bring a warm start to the autumn. Only in the second half of the month when Mercury, Venus and Mars enter Virgo is it likely to be somewhat cooler.

Northern Transplanting Time
Aug 26 to Sep 8 3ᵃ and
Sep 22 11ₚ to Oct 5
Southern Transplanting Time
Sep 8 7ₚ to Sep 22 7ₚ

The times recommended for the **fruit harvest** are those in which the Moon is in Aries or Sagittarius (Sep 7 4ᵃ to Sep 9 2ₚ, Sep 17 6ᵃ to Sep 19 4ᵃ) or other Fruit times.

The harvest of **root crops** is always best undertaken at Root times. Storage trials of onions, carrots, beetroot and potatoes have demonstrated this time and again.

Good times for **sowing winter grain** are when the Moon is in Leo or Sagittarius (Sep 7 4ᵃ to Sep 9 2ₚ, and Sep 25 1ₚ to Sep 27 8ₚ) avoiding unfavourable times, and at other Fruit times.

Rye can if necessary also be sown at Root times with all subsequent cultivations being carried out at Fruit times.

Control slugs by burning between Sep 24 2ᵃ and Sep 25 12ₚ.

Sep

Planet (naked eye) visibility
Evening: Jupiter
All night: Saturn
Morning:

Date	Const. of Moon	Solar & lunar aspects	Moon Trines	El'ment	Parts of the plant enhanced by Moon or planets	Weather

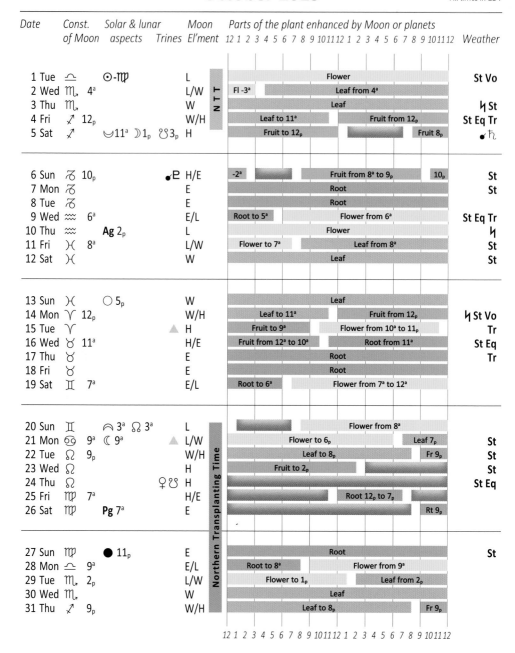

1 Tue ♎ — ☉-♍ — L — Flower — St Vo

2 Wed ♏ 4ª — L/W — Fl -3ª | Leaf from 4ª — ♄ St

3 Thu ♏ — W — Leaf — ♄ St

4 Fri ♐ 12ₚ — W/H — Leaf to 11ª | Fruit from 12ₚ — St Eq Tr

5 Sat ♐ — ☍11ª ☽1ₚ ☋3ₚ — H — Fruit to 12ₚ | Fruit 8ₚ — • ♄

6 Sun ♑ 10ₚ — • ♇ — H/E — -2ª | Fruit from 8ª to 9ₚ | 10ₚ — St

7 Mon ♑ — E — Root — St

8 Tue ♑ — E — Root

9 Wed ♒ 6ª — E/L — Root to 5ª | Flower from 6ª — St Eq Tr

10 Thu ♒ — **Ag** 2ₚ — L — Flower — ♄

11 Fri ♓ 8ª — L/W — Flower to 7ª | Leaf from 8ª — St

12 Sat ♓ — W — Leaf — St

13 Sun ♓ — ○ 5ₚ — W — Leaf

14 Mon ♈ 12ₚ — W/H — Leaf to 11ª | Fruit from 12ₚ — ♄ St Vo

15 Tue ♈ — H — Fruit to 9ª | Flower from 10ª to 11ₚ — Tr

16 Wed ♉ 11ª — H/E — Fruit from 12ₚ to 10ª | Root from 11ª — St Eq

17 Thu ♉ — E — Root — Tr

18 Fri ♉ — E — Root

19 Sat ♊ 7ª — E/L — Root to 6ª | Flower from 7ª to 12ª

20 Sun ♊ — ⌒3ª ☋3ª — L — Flower from 8ª

21 Mon ♋ 9ª ☾ 9ª — L/W — Flower to 6ₚ | Leaf 7ₚ — St

22 Tue ♌ 9ₚ — W/H — Leaf to 8ₚ | Fr 9ₚ — St

23 Wed ♌ — H — Fruit to 2ₚ — St

24 Thu ♌ — ♀☋ — H — St Eq

25 Fri ♍ 7ª — H/E — Root 12ₚ to 7ₚ

26 Sat ♍ — **Pg** 7ª — E — Rt 9ₚ

27 Sun ♍ — ● 11ₚ — E — Root — St

28 Mon ♎ 9ª — E/L — Root to 8ª | Flower from 9ª

29 Tue ♏ 2ₚ — L/W — Flower to 1ₚ | Leaf from 2ₚ

30 Wed ♏ — W — Leaf

31 Thu ♐ 9ₚ — W/H — Leaf to 8ₚ | Fr 9ₚ

(Left margin: N T T ; Northern Transplanting Time)

Time scale: 12 1 2 3 4 5 6 7 8 9 10 11 12 1 2 3 4 5 6 7 8 9 10 11 12

Mercury ☿	Venus ♀	Mars ♂	Jupiter ♃	Saturn ♄	Uranus ⛢	Neptune ♆	Pluto ♇
♍ 10 ♎	♍ 16 ♎	♍	♏	♐	♈	♒	♐
(31 R)	30 ♏				(R)	(R)	(R 3 D)

NB: All zodiac symbols refer to astronomical constellations, not astrological signs (see p. 24)

(Left vertical tab: Oct)

Even though Saturn, Uranus and Pluto remain in Warmth constellations, the presence of Mercury, Venus and Mars in the Earth constellation of Virgo is likely to at least balance them out. When Venus and Mercury move into Libra in the middle of the month a bright autumnal period will arrive.

Northern Transplanting Time
Sep 22 to Oct 5 9ᵃ and
Oct 20 5ᵃ to Nov 1
Southern Transplanting Time
Oct 5 1ₚ to Oct 20 1ᵃ

Store fruit at any Fruit or Flower time outside transplanting time.

Harvest seeds of root plants at Root times, **seeds for leaf plants** at Leaf times, and **seeds for flower plants** at Flower times.

All **cleared ground** should be treated with compost and sprayed with barrel preparation, and plowed ready for winter.

Control slugs by burning between Oct 21 9ᵃ and Oct 22 8ₚ.

Biodynamic preparations (Maria Thun's tree log preparations): Cut **larch** and fill with chamomile and put it in the ground between Oct 7 2ᵃ and 8ᵃ. Put **birch** and yarrow into the ground on Oct 12 between 10ᵃ to 6ₚ.

Day	Aspects
1	
2	
3	☽ ☌ ♃ 5ₚ
4	
5	☽ ● ♄ 5ₚ
6	☽ ● ♇ 5ᵃ
7	☿ ☍ ♁ 2ᵃ
8	
9	
10	☽ ☌ ♆ 10ₚ
11	
12	☽ ☍ ♂ 12ₚ ♀ ☍ ♁ 6ₚ
13	
14	☾ ☌ ♁ 10ₚ
15	☾ ☍ ♀ 5ₚ ☿ △ ♆ 7ₚ ☾ ☍ ☿ 9ₚ
16	
17	
18	☾ ☍ ♃ 2ᵃ
19	
20	☾ ☍ ♄ 10ᵃ ☾ ☍ ♇ 8ₚ
21	♀ △ ♆ 4ₚ
22	
23	
24	☾ ☍ ♆ 6ₚ ♀ ☍ 11ₚ
25	
26	☾ ☌ ♂ 4ₚ
27	☾ ☍ ♁ 11ₚ
28	☉ ☍ ♁ 4ᵃ
29	☽ ☌ ♀ 11ᵃ ☽ ☌ ☿ 2ₚ
30	☿ ☌ ♀ 6ₚ
31	☽ ☌ ♃ 11ᵃ

Planet (naked eye) visibility
Evening: Venus (from 12th), Jupiter, Saturn
All night:
Morning: Mars (from 16th)

Oct

▬▬▬▬ *Unfavourable time* 51

November 2019

All times in EDT / EST

Date	Const. of Moon		Solar & lunar aspects	Trines	Moon El'ment	Parts of the plant enhanced by Moon or planets (12 1 2 3 4 5 6 7 8 9 10 11 12 1 2 3 4 5 6 7 8 9 10 11 12)	Weather
1 Fri	♐		☉-♍ ☋6_p ◡8_p		H	Fruit to 3_p	St Tr
2 Sat	♐		☉-♎	☌♄ ☌♇	H	Fr 6^a - 11^a; Fruit from 5_p	St
DST ends in North America							
*All times below in **EST***							
3 Sun	♑	4^a			H/E	-3^a EST; Root from 4^a	
4 Mon	♑		☽ 5^a		E	Root	St
5 Tue	♒	12_p			E/L	Root to 11^a; Flower from 12_p	St Vo
6 Wed	♒				L	Flower	St Vo
7 Thu	♓	2_p	**Ag** 4^a		L/W	Flower to 1_p; Leaf from 2_p	St Eq
8 Fri	♓			▲	W	Lf -3^a; Flower 4^a - 4_p; Leaf from 5_p	
9 Sat	♓				W	Leaf	ϟ St
10 Sun	♈	7_p			W/H	Leaf to 8^a	
11 Mon	♈			☌☿ ☿☊	H	11	St
12 Tue	♉	4_p	○ 9^a		H/E	Fruit to 3_p; Root to 4_p	St
13 Wed	♉			▲	E	Root to 7^a; Flower from 8^a to 9_p; 10_p	
14 Thu	♉				E	Root	St Vo
15 Fri	♊	11^a			E/L	Root to 10^a; Flower from 11^a	
16 Sat	♊		☊ 4^a ⌒ 8^a		L	1^a; Flower from 9^a	
17 Sun	♋	1_p			L/W	Flower to 12_p; Leaf from 1_p	ϟ St
18 Mon	♋				W	Leaf	St
19 Tue	♌	2^a	☾ 4_p		W/H	1^a; Fruit from 2^a	
20 Wed	♌		☉-♏		H	Fruit	St
21 Thu	♍	1_p			H/E	Fruit to 12_p; Root from 1_p	
22 Fri	♍				E	Root to 3_p	
23 Sat	♍		**Pg** 3^a		E	Root from 5_p	St
24 Sun	♎	6_p			E/L	Root to 5_p; Flower from 6_p	St
25 Mon	♎				L/W	Flower to 11_p	
26 Tue	♏	12^a	● 10^a		W	Leaf from 12^a	
27 Wed	♏				W	Leaf to 7_p; Fl 8_p	Tr
28 Thu	♐	5^a	*Thanksgiving* ☋11_p		W/H	Fl -3^a; Fruit 9^a to 8_p (sp good 6^a-3_p)	▲▲ ☌♃
29 Fri	♐		◡ 5^a	☌♄ ☌♇	H	Fruit from 4^a to 1_p	Tr
30 Sat	♑	1_p			H/E	Fruit from 2^a to 12_p; Root from 1_p	

Northern Transplanting Time (16–28 Nov)

Nov

Mercury ☿	Venus ♀	Mars ♂	Jupiter ♃	Saturn ♄	Uranus ♅	Neptune ♆	Pluto ♇
♎	♏	♍	♏	♐	♈	♒	♐
(R 20 D)	24 ♐		26 ♐		(R)	(R 27 D)	

NB: All zodiac symbols refer to astronomical constellations, not astrological signs (see p. 24)

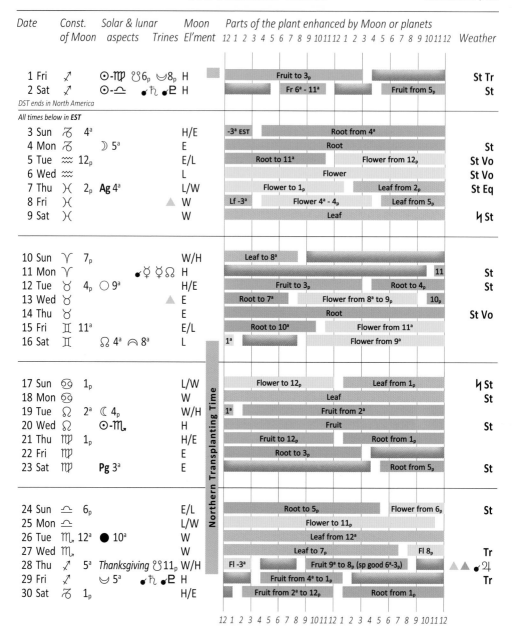

Planetary aspects
(**Bold** = *visible to naked eye)*

1
2 **☽●♄ 3^a** ☽●♇ 2_p
3
4
5
6
7 ☽☌♆ 3^a
8 ☉△♆ 1_p
9
10 ☽☍♂ 7^a
11 ☽☌♅ 2^a ☿☊ 9^a ☉●☿ 10^a
12 ☽☍☿ 5^a
13 ☿△♆ 5_p
14 ☾☍♀ 9^a
15 ☾☍♃ 4^a
16 ☾☍♄ 5_p
17 ☾☍♇ 1^a
18
19
20 ☾☍♆ 11_p
21
22
23
24 **☾☌♂ 7^a** ☾☍♅ 7^a **♀☌♃ 9^a** ♂☍♅ 12_p **☾☌☿ 11_p**
25
26
27
28 ☿△♆ 5^a **☽●♃ 6^a** ♀△♅ 1_p **☽☌♀ 2_p**
29 **☽●♄ 4_p** ☽●♇ 11_p
30

Planet (naked eye) visibility
Evening: Venus, Jupiter, Saturn
All night:
Morning: Mercury (from 19th), Mars

November 2019

Although it is unclear whether Mars in the cooler constellation of Virgo or Saturn in the warmth of Sagittarius will take precedence, the Light trines and the presence of Mercury in Libra will at least ensure some brightness. With Venus and Jupiter in Scorpio we can expect November to be wet.

Northern Transplanting Time
Oct 20 to Nov 1 6_p
Nov 16 10^a to Nov 29 3^a
Southern Transplanting Time
Nov 1 10_p to Nov 16 6^a and
Nov 29 7^a to Dec 13

The Flower times in Transplanting Time are ideal for **planting flower bulbs,** showing vigorous growth and vivid colours. The remaining Flower times should only be considered as back up, as bulbs planted on those times will not flower so freely.

If not already completed in October, all organic waste materials should be gathered and made into a **compost.** Applying the biodynamic preparations to the compost will ensure a rapid transformation and good fungal development. An application of barrel preparation will also help the composting process.

Fruit and forest trees will also benefit at this time from a spraying of horn manure and/or barrel preparation when being transplanted.

Best times for **cutting Advent greenery** and **Christmas trees** for transporting are Flower times, avoiding unfavourable times).

Burn **fly papers** in cow barn at Flower times.

Biodynamic preparations
Maria Thun's tree log preparations: Cut **oak,** fill it with coarsely ground oak bark and put it in the earth on Nov 24 between 9^a and 4_p.

Unfavourable time

December 2019

All times in EST

Date	Const. of Moon		Solar & lunar aspects	Trines	Moon El'ment	Parts of the plant enhanced by Moon or planets (12 1 2 3 4 5 6 7 8 9 10 11 12 1 2 3 4 5 6 7 8 9 10 11 12)	Weather
1 Sun	♑		☉-♏		E	Root	♄ St
2 Mon	♒	8_p			E/L	Root to 7_p; Fl 8_p	
3 Tue	♒				L	Flower	Tr
4 Wed	♓	10_p	☽ 2^a **Ag** 11_p		L/W	Flower	St
5 Thu	♓				W	Fl -3^a; Leaf from 4^a	St
6 Fri	♓				W	Leaf	
7 Sat	♓				W	Leaf	
8 Sun	♈	2^a			W/H	1^a; Fruit from 2^h	St Eq Vo
9 Mon	♈				H	Fruit to 11_p	
10 Tue	♉	12^a			E	Root from 12^a	♄ St
11 Wed	♉				E	Root	
12 Thu	♊	6_p	○ 1^a		E/L	Root to 5_p; Fl 6_p (sp gd 8_p)	St
13 Fri	♊		☊ 9^a ⋒ 3_p	▲	L	Fl (sp good) -6^a; Flower from 2_p	
14 Sat	♋	7_p			L/W	Flower to 6_p; Leaf 7_p	St Vo
15 Sun	♋			▲	W	-2^a; Fruit from 3^a to 5_p; Leaf from 7_p	♄ St
16 Mon	♌	7^a			W/H	Leaf to 6^a; Fruit from 7^a	St
17 Tue	♌				H	Fruit	
18 Wed	♍	7_p	**Pg** 3_p ☾ 11_p		H/E	Fr -3^h	St
19 Thu	♍			☿☋	E		
20 Fri	♍		☉-♐		E	Root from 5^a	St Eq Vo Tr
21 Sat	♍				E	Root to 12^a	♄ St Eq
22 Sun	♎	1^a			L	Flower from 1^a	♄ St
23 Mon	♏	8^a			L/W	Flower to 7^a; Leaf from 8^a	
24 Tue	♏			▲	W	Leaf to 5^a; Fruit from 6^a from 8_p; Lf 9_p	Tr
25 Wed	♐	3_p	*Christmas*		W/H	Leaf to 2_p; Fruit 3_p to 10_p	
26 Thu	♐		☉☌● 1^a ☋ 8^a ◡ 2_p		H	Fruit from 1_p	☌♃ Tr
27 Fri	♐	10_p		☌♇	H/E	Fruit to 7^a; Fruit from 1_p to 9_p; 10_p	
28 Sat	♑			☌♀	E	Root to 6_p	St Eq
29 Sun	♑				E	Root from 12^a	
30 Mon	♒	4^a		▲	E/L	Rt -3^a; Fl 4^a-7^a; Fruit from 8^a to 9_p; 10_p	St
31 Tue	♒				L	Flower	Tr

Northern Transplanting Time

Mercury ☿	Venus ♀	Mars ♂	Jupiter ♃	Saturn ♄	Uranus ♅	Neptune ♆	Pluto ♇
♎ 7 ♏	♐	♍ 3 ♎	♐	♐	♈	♒	♐
28 ♐	19 ♑	30 ♏			(R)		

NB: All zodiac symbols refer to astronomical constellations, not astrological signs (see p. 24)

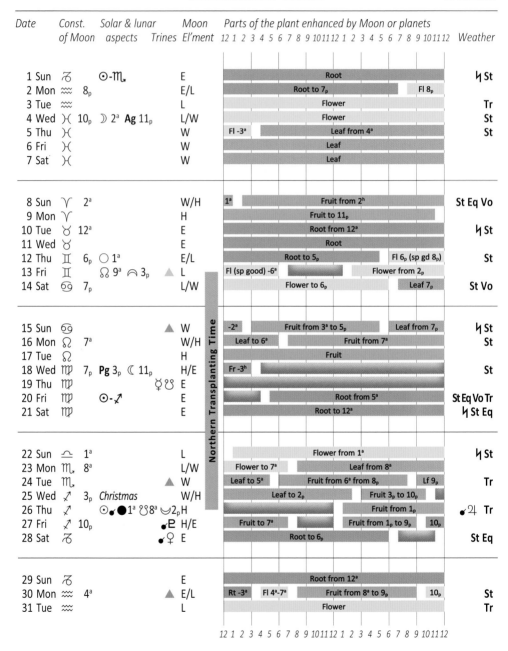

Planetary aspects

December 2019

We can unfortunately not hope for a white Christmas. Three Warmth trines one of which occurs on Christmas Eve as well as several planets in Warmth constellations will preclude any really cold weather. New Year's Eve is also likely to be mild thanks to Mercury which enters Sagittarius on December 28.

1	
2	
3	
4	☽☌♆ 10ᵃ
5	
6	
7	

8	☽☌☊ 9ᵃ
9	☽☍♂ 4ᵃ
10	☽☍☿ 4ₚ
11	♀☌♄ 5ᵃ
12	☾☍♃ 11ₚ
13	♂△♆ 7ᵃ ♀☌♇ 10ᵃ
14	☾☌♄ 5ᵃ ☾☍♇ 9ᵃ ☾☍♀ 11ᵃ

15	♃△☊ 2ₚ
16	
17	
18	☾☍♆ 6ᵃ
19	☿☊ 4ₚ
20	
21	☾☍☊ 1ₚ

22	☾☌♂ 10ₚ
23	
24	☉△☊ 5ₚ
25	☾☌☿ 6ᵃ
26	☽•♃ 3ᵃ
27	☽☌♄ 7ᵃ ☽•♇ 10ᵃ ☉☌♃ 1ₚ
28	☽•♀ 9ₚ

29	
30	☿△☊ 5ₚ
31	☽☌♆ 7ₚ

Northern Transplanting Time
Dec 13 5ₚ to Dec 26 12ₚ
Southern Transplanting Time
Nov 29 to Dec 13 1ₚ and
Dec 26 4ₚ to Jan 9

The transplanting time is good for **pruning trees and hedges.** Fruit trees should be pruned at Fruit or Flower times.

Best times for cutting **Advent greenery** and **Christmas trees** are at Flower times to ensure lasting fragrance.

Southern hemisphere:
Harvest time for seeds (always avoiding unfavourable times**):**
Leaf seeds: Leaf times.
Fruit seeds: Fruit times, preferably with Moon in Leo (Dec 16 7ᵃ to Dec 18 3ᵃ).
Root seeds: Dec 20 5ᵃ to Dec 21 11ₚ, and at other Root times.
Flower seeds: Dec 12 6ₚ to Dec 14 6ₚ, and at other Flower times.

Control slugs Dec 14 7ₚ to Dec 16 6ᵃ.

We wish all our readers a blessed holiday time and the best of health for the New Year of 2020

Planet (naked eye) visibility
Evening: Venus, Jupiter (to 11th), Saturn (to 28th)
All night:
Morning: Mercury (to 18th), Mars

Sowing times for trees and shrubs

June 14: Yew, Oak, Hornbeam, Cherry, Horse chestnut (buckeye), Sweet chestnut, Spruce, Fir

June 16: Ash, Cedar, Fir, Spruce, Hazel, Lime tree, Elm, Thuja, Juniper, Plum, Hornbeam

June 19 (14^h–22^h): Alder, Larch, Lime tree, Elm, Juniper, Plum

June 23: Maple, Apple, Apricot, Birch, Pear, Hornbeam, Lime tree, Mirabelle plum, Peach, Plum, Robinia, Thuja, Juniper, Willow

July 17: Pear, Birch, Lime tree, Robinia, Willow, Thuja, Juniper, Plum, Hornbeam

July 21: Birch, Pear, Lime tree, Robinia, Willow, Thuja, Juniper, Plum, Hornbeam

Sep 10: Ash, Spruce, Hazel, Fir, Cedar

Oct 7: Alder, Larch, Lime tree, Elm

Oct 28: Ash, Cedar, Fir, Spruce, Hazel

Sowing times depend on planetary aspects and are not specific to either northern or southern hemispheres. For trees and shrubs not mentioned above, sow at an appropriate time of the Moon's position in the zodiac, depending on the part of the tree or shrub to be enhanced. Avoid unfavourable times.

Sowing times are different from transplanting times. Seedlings should be transplanted during the descending Moon when the Moon is in a constellation corresponding to the part of the tree to to be enhanced. It is important to remember that seedlings need to be sufficiently mature to withstand the winter. The time of sowing should therefore chime in with local conditions and take account of the germination habit of each tree species.

Felling times for timber

Feb 3: Birch, Pear, Larch, Lime tree, Robinia, Willow

May 9: Birch, Pear, Robinia, Willow, Maple, Apple, Copper beech, Sweet chestnut, Walnut

June 16: Alder, Larch, Lime tree, Elm

Aug 7: Ash, Spruce, Hazel, Fir, Cedar

Aug 9: Birch, Pear, Robinia, Willow, Maple, Apple, Copper beech, Sweet chestnut, Walnut

Aug 21: Alder, Larch, Lime tree, Elm

Sep 1: Alder, Larch, Lime tree, Elm, Birch, Pear, Robinia, Willow, Maple, Apple, Copper beech, Sweet chestnut, Walnut

Sep 19: Yew, Oak, Cherry, Sweet chestnut, Horse chestnut (buckeye)

Nov 17: Alder, Larch, Lime tree, Elm

Nov 28: Birch, Pear, Larch, Lime tree, Robinia, Willow

Dec 24: Ash, Spruce, Hazel, Fir, Cedar

Dec 30: Maple, Apple, Copper beech, Sweet chestnut, Walnut, Spruce, Hornbeam, Pine, Fir, Thuja, Cedar, Plum

Those trees which are not listed should be felled at the end of the growing season at Flower times during the descending Moon period (transplanting time). Avoid unfavourable times.

Types of crop

Flower plants

artichoke
broccoli
flower bulbs
flowering ornamental shrubs
flowers
flowery herbs
rose
sunflower

Leaf plants

asparagus
Brussels sprouts
cabbage
cauliflower
celery
chard
chicory (endive)
Chinese cabbage (pe-tsai)
corn salad (lamb's lettuce)
crisphead (iceberg) lettuce
curly kale (green cabbage)
endive (chicory)
finocchio (Florence fennel)
green cabbage (curly kale)
iceberg (crisphead) lettuce
kohlrabi
lamb's lettuce (corn salad)
leaf herbs
leek
lettuce
pe-tsai (Chinese cabbage)
red cabbage
rhubarb
shallots
spinach

Root plants

beetroot
black (Spanish) salsify
carrot
celeriac
garlic
horseradish
Jerusalem artichoke
parsnip
potato
radish
red radish
root tubers
Spanish (black) salsify

Fruit plants

aubergine (eggplant)
bush bean
courgette (zucchini)
cucumber
eggplant (aubergine)
grains
lentil
maize
melon
paprika
pea
pumpkin (squash)
runner bean
soya
squash (pumpkin)
tomato
zucchini (courgette)

The care of bees

A colony of bees lives in its hive closed off from the outside world. For extra protection against harmful influences, the inside of the hive is sealed with propolis. The link with the wider surroundings is made by the bees that fly in and out of the hive.

To make good use of cosmic rhythms, the beekeeper needs to create the right conditions in much the same way as the gardener or farmer does with the plants. The gardener works the soil and in so doing allows cosmic forces to penetrate it via the air. These forces can then be taken up and used by the plants until the soil is next moved.

When the beekeeper opens up the hive, the sealing layer of propolis is broken. This creates a disturbance, as a result of which cosmic forces can enter and influence the life of the hive until the next intervention by the beekeeper. By this means the beekeeper can directly mediate cosmic forces to the bees.

It is not insignificant which forces of the universe are brought into play when the the hive is opened. The beekeeper can consciously intervene by choosing days for working with the hive that will help the colony to develop and build up its food reserves. The bees will then reward the beekeeper by providing a portion of their harvest in the form of honey.

Earth-Root times can be selected for opening the hive if the bees need to do more building. Light-Flower times encourage brood activity and colony development. Warmth-Fruit times stimulate the collection of nectar. Water-Leaf times are unsuitable for working in the hive or for the removal and processing of honey.

Since the late 1970s the varroa mite has affected virtually every bee colony in Europe. Following a number of comparative trials we recommend burning and making an ash of the varroa mite in the usual way. After dynamizing it for one hour, the ash should be put in a salt-cellar and sprinkled lightly between the combs. The ash should be made and sprinkled when the Sun and Moon are in Taurus (May/June).

Feeding bees in preparation for winter

The herbal teas recommended as supplements in the feeding of bees prior to winter are all plants that have proved their value over many years. Yarrow, chamomile, dandelion and valerian are made by pouring boiling water over the flowers, allowing them to brew for fifteen minutes and then straining them. Stinging nettle, horsetail and oak bark are placed in cold water, brought slowly to the boil and simmered for fifteen minutes. Three grams (1 tablespoon) of each dried herb and half a litre (½ quart) of the prepared teas is enough to produce 100 litres (25 gal) of liquid feed. This is a particularly important treatment in years when there are large amounts of honeydew.

Fungal problems

The function of fungus in nature is to break down dying organic materials. It appears amongst our crops when unripe manure compost or uncomposted animal by-products such as horn and bone meal are used but also when seeds are harvested during unfavourable constellations: according to Steiner, 'When Moon forces are working too strongly on the Earth ...'

Tea can be made from horsetail (*Equisetum arvense*) and sprayed on to the soil where affected plants are growing. This draws the fungal level back down into the ground where it belongs.

The plants can be strengthened by spraying stinging nettle tea on the leaves. This will promote good assimilation, stimulate the flow of sap and help fungal diseases to disappear.

Biodynamic preparation plants

Pick **dandelions** in the morning at Flower times as soon as they are open and while the centre of the flowers are still tightly packed.

Pick **yarrow** at Fruit times when the Sun is in Leo (around the middle of August).

Pick **chamomile** at Flower times just before midsummer. If they are harvested too late, seeds will begin to form and there are often grubs in the hollow heads.

Collect **stinging nettles** when the first flowers are opening, usually around midsummer. Harvest the whole plants without roots at Flower times.

Pick **valerian** at Flower times around midsummer.

All the flowers (except valerian) should be laid out on paper and dried in the shade.

Collect **oak bark** at Root times. The pithy material below the bark should not be used.

Moon diagrams

The diagrams overleaf show for each month the daily position (evenings GMT) of the Moon against the stars and other planets. For viewing in the southern hemisphere, turn the diagrams upside down.

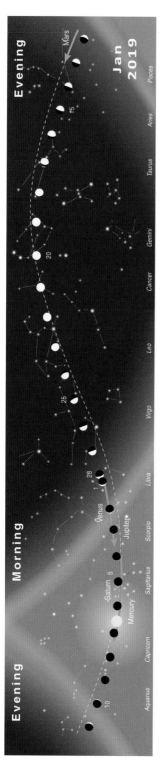

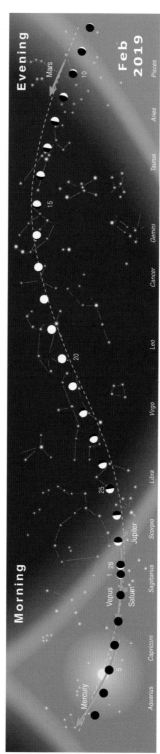

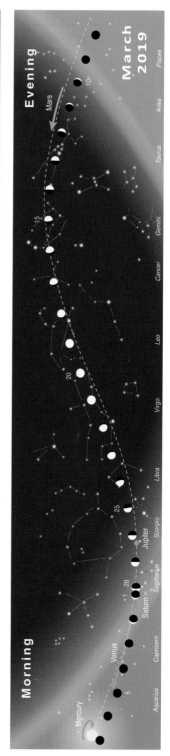

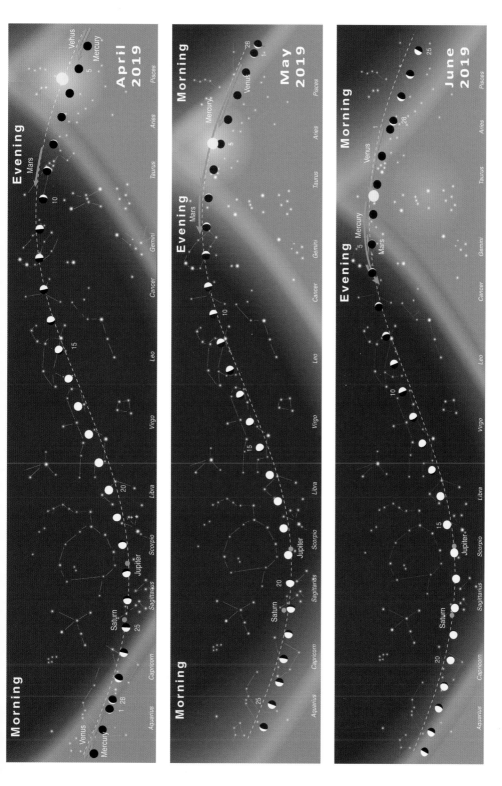

Evening

Venus
Mercury
Mars
Pisces
Aries
Taurus
Gemini
Cancer
Leo
Virgo
Libra
Scorpio
Jupiter
Sagittarius
Saturn
Capricorn
Aquarius
Venus
Mercury

April 2019

Morning

Morning

Mercury
Venus
Pisces
Aries
Taurus
Gemini
Cancer
Leo
Virgo
Libra
Scorpio
Jupiter
Sagittarius
Saturn
Capricorn
Aquarius

Evening

Mars

May 2019

Morning

Morning

Venus
Pisces
Aries
Taurus
Mercury
Gemini
Cancer
Mars
Leo
Virgo
Libra
Scorpio
Jupiter
Sagittarius
Saturn
Capricorn
Aquarius

Evening

June 2019

61

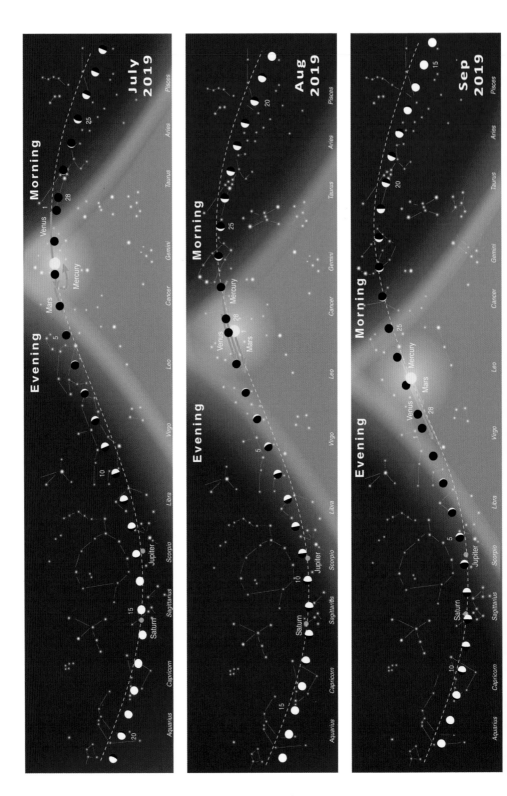

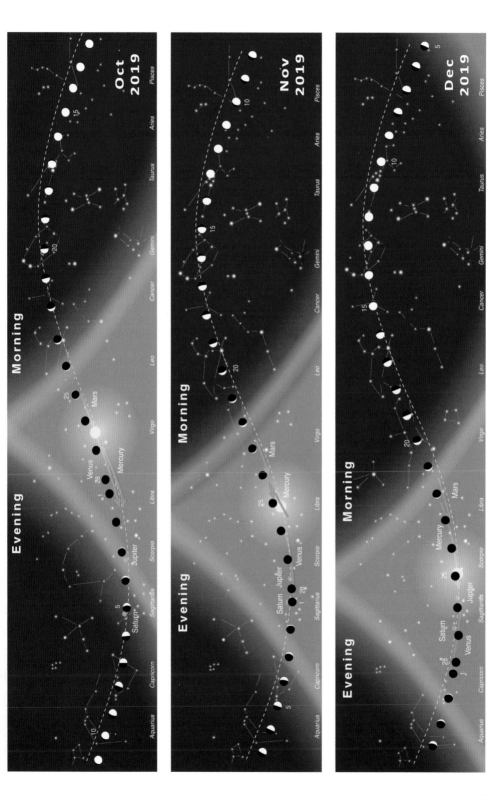

Further Reading

Colquhoun, Margaret and Axel Ewald, *New Eyes for Plants,* Hawthorn

Karlsson, Britt and Per, *Biodynamic, Organic and Natural Winemaking,* Floris

Klett, Manfred, *Principles of Biodynamic Spray and Compost Preparations,* Floris

Klocek, Dennis, *Sacred Agriculture: The Alchemy of Biodynamics,* Lindisfarne

Koepf, H.H., *Koepf's Practical Biodynamics: Soil, Compost, Sprays and Food Quality,* Floris

König, Karl, *Social Farming: Healing Humanity and the Earth,* Floris

Kranich, Ernst Michael, *Planetary Influences upon Plants,* Biodynamic Association, USA

Lepetit, Antoine, *What's so Special About Biodynamic Wine?* Floris

Masson, Pierre, *A Biodynamic Manual,* Floris

Morrow, Joel, *Vegetable Gardening for Organic and Biodynamic Growers,* Lindisfarne

Osthaus, K.-E., *The Biodynamic Farm,* Floris

Pfeiffer, Ehrenfried, *The Earth's Face,* Lanthorn

—, *Pfeiffer's Introduction to Biodynamics,* Floris

—, *Weeds and What They Tell Us,* Floris

—, & Michael Maltas, *The Biodynamic Orchard Book,* Floris

Philbrick, John and Helen, *Gardening for Health and Nutrition,* Anthroposophic, USA

Philbrick, Helen & Gregg, Richard B., *Companion Plants and How to Use Them,* Floris

Sattler, Friedrich & Eckard von Wistinghausen, *Growing Biodynamic Crops,* Floris

Schilthuis, Willy, *Biodynamic Agriculture,* Floris

Steiner, Rudolf, *Agriculture (A Course of Eight Lectures),* Biodynamic Association, USA

—, *Agriculture: An Introductory Reader,* Steiner Press, UK

—, *What is Biodynamics? A Way to Heal and Revitalize the Earth,* SteinerBooks, USA

Storl, Wolf, *Culture and Horticulture,* North Atlantic Books, USA

Thun, Maria, *Gardening for Life,* Hawthorn

—, *The Biodynamic Year,* Temple Lodge

Thun, Matthias, *When Wine Tastes Best: A Biodynamic Calendar for Wine Drinkers,* (annual) Floris

von Keyserlink, Adelbert Count, *The Birth of a New Agriculture,* Temple Lodge

—, *Developing Biodynamic Agriculture,* Temple Lodge

Weiler, Michael, *Bees and Honey, from Flower to Jar,* Floris

Wright, Hilary, *Biodynamic Gardening for Health and Taste,* Floris

Biodynamic Associations

Demeter International
www.demeter.net
Australia:
Bio-Dynamic Research Institute
www.demeter.org.au
Biodynamic Agriculture Australia
www.biodynamics.net.au
Canada: Society for Bio-Dynamic Farming & Gardening in Ontario
biodynamics.on.ca
India: Bio-Dynamic Association of India (BDAI)
www.biodynamics.in

Ireland: Biodynamic Agriculture Association of Ireland
www.biodynamicagriculture.ie
New Zealand:
NZ Biodynamic Association
www.biodynamic.org.nz
South Africa: Biodynamic Agricultural Association of Southern Africa
www.bdaasa.org.za
UK: Biodynamic Association
www.biodynamic.org.uk
USA: Biodynamic Association
www.biodynamics.com